The Lesbian Couples' Guide

The Lesbian Couples Guide

McDaniel, Judith

Also by Judith McDaniel

Metamorphosis
Sanctuary
Just Say Yes

The Lesbian Couples' Guide

Finding the Right Woman and Creating a Life Together

Judith McDaniel

 **HarperPerennial**
A Division of HarperCollins Publishers

HarperCollins books may be purchased for educational, business, or sales promotional use. For information please write: Special Markets Department, HarperCollins Publishers, Inc., 10 East 53rd Street, New York, NY 10022.

Designed by C. Linda Dingler

ISBN 0-06-095021-8

95 96 97 98 99 ❖/HC 10 9 8 7 6 5 4 3 2

for Jan
with my love

Contents

PART VIII: UNCOUPLING

PART IX: GOING LONG TERM

Acknowledgments

I would like to thank the many friends who helped and supported me while I was writing this book. Some have asked not to be named, but each will recognize, I believe, her own contribution.

Thank you to the many women who read this book at different stages:

Bernice Mennis, one of my most valued readers and critics; Judith Mazza, who keeps me on track; and Paula Sawyer, Phyllis Rusnock, Edella Schlager, Patricia Holland, Karen Holloway, and Judie Mut, who each brought her experience to read and question.

Thank you to those who gave me ideas before this book began and information as it was progressing:

Pam McFall, Anna Bulkin, Joanie Trussel, Meghan Stahlke, Maureen O'Brien, Becky Smith, Harmony Hammond, Alice DeBuhr, Jill Bielawski, Barbara Smith, Cindy Colen, Pat Hughes, and Charlotte Sheedy, agent and friend, all three of my editors at HarperCollins, and many others who cannot be named.

Thank you to my community, including Antigone Books, Tucson's wonderful women's bookstore; Wingspan, our gay/lesbian community center; and to Margaret Avery Moon and my friends at The Desert Institute of the Healing Arts.

Special thanks to my family, Jan, Adam, Barbara—who were here in Tucson for the writing; to Erica, Peggy, Cathy, Bruce, and the nieces and nephews who are a positive force in my life.

And to the memory of my father, Ralph McDaniel, who thought this book was a wonderful idea, and my friend Mary Catherine, who contributed in vital ways. I miss you both.

While a community of women contributed to this book, I alone am responsible for its direction and execution, including any errors, outrages, or misstatements.

PART ONE

Defining Ourselves

Introduction

I was sitting in a bar with a friend in the early seventies. It was St. Patrick's Day and we were trying to ignore the party happening on the other side of the room. I was talking intently to this woman friend, talking intimately. We were very involved in one another and it wasn't hard to ignore the other bar patrons. Until one of them staggered up to our booth, looked us up and down lecherously, and asked, "Are you girls alone?" Without thought, and certainly without preparation, I looked him dead in the eye and replied, "No, we're together." We were. Two women together. He didn't know what to make of my reply, scratched his head for a moment, then wandered back to his friends, muttering, "Together. They say they're together." And we were.

When I first began to consider writing a book about and for lesbian couples, for two women together, I wondered what I could say that would be of interest to the wide spectrum of women who are lesbians, women who are as different from one another as any fantasist could possibly imagine, except in one crucial way: we all choose women as our life partners, our intimate partners, our sexual partners. That choice, its joys, puzzles, and difficulties, is what this book is about.

I define the term *lesbian* in the context of self-knowledge and self-definition. Do I know myself and my desires as lesbian? Do I describe myself as lesbian? A woman who so describes herself may choose a woman for her sexual partner. She may want and find a life partner, or she may not ever want to live with another woman. A woman who is a lesbian may choose a woman for her life partner and never be sexual with her or any other woman. A woman who is a lesbian may find her primary social satisfaction in the company of other lesbians, or she may not. The reverse is also true. Women who are not lesbians can and have lived together companionably for decades. Women who are not lesbians have sometimes chosen other women for sexual partners. I don't think we need to describe those women's reality for them; nor do we need to assume that they are only responding to internalized homophobia and/or self-hatred in denying they are lesbian.

I am a lesbian. I have known myself and my desires in that way since before I had a name for the feelings. In my teens and twenties, by and large I succeeded in suppressing those feelings and presenting a heterosexual front to myself and the world. Not until I was thirty did I figure out how to act on those feelings, but I've been acting on them now for more than twenty years. Today I live with Jan, my lover, in a committed, monogamous relationship. Several years ago we decided to make a public statement about our relationship and had a Quaker wedding in which we spoke our commitment to one another in the presence of our friends and families.

I am also a white middle-class, academically trained, self-employed lesbian. The women I share values and community with do not all fit that description. I have never owned a motorcycle or gotten a tattoo or been to a women/lesbian music festival or tried s/m sex. Some of my lovers and friends have. These are not the issues that would divide my community. The women in my community may have different tastes than I, may find their excitement in different places than I, but they are women who respect their own choices and the choices of others.

"I am large . . . " said gay poet Walt Whitman in 1855, "I contain multitudes." So also does that entity we refer to as "the lesbian community," as though it had a single identity. A strong lesbian community means not just acknowledging our diversity, but encouraging and celebrating it. And a healthy diversity means welcoming into this lesbian community the lipstick lesbians, the dykes on bikes, the butch/femme couples, the s/m players, the wimmin on the land who want to build a blood hut to celebrate menstrual cycles, the academic lesbian professors, and all the varieties of lesbians who arrive at their sexual orientation in the context of a racial/cultural community: the Asian American lesbians, African American lesbians, Native American lesbians, the Irish Catholic lesbian nuns, and many, many more lesbian communities.

Recently, lesbians have been brought more into the consciousness of Middle America—the covers of *Newsweek*, *Vanity Fair*, on sitcoms like *Roseanne* and in films like *Orlando*. While the closet can be a dark and guilt-ridden place, there are days when it's starting to look like a haven. Did you ever expect to hear Barbara Walters explaining the difference between butch and femme? The dangers of being chic and of being demonized are opposite sides of one coin. Others still have the power to define us, to name us to ourselves, and in that describing, they can shape our lives. We need to take that power for ourselves; we need to describe our own lives.

I hope this book will help *us* to look with new eyes at the realities of lesbian couples. We all—new lesbians and experienced ones, couples of a few days and of many years—need to be reminded both that loving other women puts us off most psychological and sociological "norm" charts *and* that women have been loving one another like this for years, for centuries. We can learn some lessons from our history—both recent and distant.

Being aware of the issues is a major step toward personal growth and community development. It can also be terrifying, or at least anxiety producing, because most often awareness puts us in a new place, foreign territory. I like to think of *The Lesbian Couples' Guide* as a new kind of road map, one that will take us to places we've always wanted to go and show us a few of the best tourist highlights on the way.

Finding the Past,
Creating the Future

Women have always chosen one another for lovers, companions, intimate friends. While for our lives in our times I define *lesbian* in terms of self-knowledge and self-definition, women who were lesbians in other times may not have named themselves or their relationships. And because those relationships were unnamed or were called by names meant to disguise rather than reveal their nature, it was possible to assume that lesbians didn't exist before the middle part of the twentieth century. They did exist, of course, in spite of the often repeated apocryphal story about why only male homosexuality was banned in England in the nineteenth century: Queen Victoria couldn't imagine what two women might *do* together and so refused to entertain outlawing something that could not exist. At least, that's the story I've heard.

In *Surpassing the Love of Men: Romantic Friendship and Love Between Women from the Renaissance to the Present,*[1] Lillian Faderman examines the cult of "passionate friendships" between women, excavating beneath the surface representation for suggestions—or evidence—that lesbians existed before the term *lesbian* came into being as a cultural, psychological, and medical creation. If the term *lesbian* today means more than sex, which I insist that it does, is it important whether or not our historical predecessors did or did not engage in genital sexual contact? Yes, I think so. Look at nineteenth-century history. An entire culture proclaimed that women had no sexual desire of any description and that allowing her husband to have sexual access was a woman's unpleasant and necessary duty, but why should we today perpetuate that Victorian falsehood? We know better. So did many Victorians. We can't, of course, say which Victorian women couples were having hot, satisfying genital contact and which weren't. As Faderman and Carroll Smith-Rosenberg[2] have pointed out, romantic expressions of undying eternal love to a female friend were both fashionable and allowed to our great-great-grandmothers. We cannot presume that those expressions had the same meaning then that they would have today. As the anecdote about Queen Victoria illustrates, the commonly held view of sexuality in the nineteenth century was that sex was something penises did. Our lesbian foremothers may have been having what we consider sex, but they might not have named it that. Nonetheless, I don't think we should deny the full potential of their loving, the full range of expression of that loving.

That some of those relationships were, in fact, more than "romantic friendships" was documented by Judith C. Brown in 1982, when she discovered an obscure document detailing the trial of a nun in Renaissance Italy who was involved in a specifically sexual relationship with another nun.[3] The ecclesiastical investigation into the case of Abbess Benedetta Carlini dates from the years 1619-23 and is extraordinary because it is the only one of thousands of same-sex cases, tried by lay and ecclesiastical authorities during this period, that involved women.[4] According to the transcript, Benedetta imagined herself in the form of a male angel she called Splendidiello when she made love to the nun whose testimony convicted her—an image that simultaneously startles me with its bold assertion and saddens me. I wonder what she truly thought or felt when she bent her head "to put her face between the other's breasts and kiss them."[5]

And yet, however different the assumptions and conditions of the lives of our foremothers seem to me, it is also clear that the "female world of varied and yet highly structured relationships"[6] holds information we need today as we reinvent the possibilities for ourselves as lesbian couples. One lesson is simple: attitudes of the dominant society do change. What is "common wisdom" or "infallible truth" today may seem ludicrous tomorrow. If nothing else, the realization that lesbians in the twenty-first century may look at our lives with raised eyebrows and incredulous faces ought to give us a certain leniency of attitude—not only toward our foremothers, but also toward those lesbians in our own societies who are being lesbians differently than we, whatever in-groups "we" consist of at any given moment. But I also find a certain comfort in knowing that homophobic attitudes can and have changed, because I'm an optimist and live as though I were sure these attitudes will change for the better. Today's issue may be whether or not being homosexual and serving in the military are "compatible" or not; but we can be sure it won't be tomorrow's issue.

When I read about the lives of historical women who chose women for their life companions, I am awed by the variety of structures that accommodated their loving. Some lived as nuns in all-women communities and cherished "special friends" in the context of community. Some lived as wives and mothers and cherished "romantic friends." Others chose adventure, dressing and living as men with their wives. A few lived in ménages, multiple-relationship families, the intricacies of which we can only guess at today. Some were the first professional women, garnering support from loving, lifelong relationships for the difficult journey into a previously all-male world. Our foremothers showed us one important lesson through their lives and struggles—that there was no one correct way to be with a woman companion. They found relationships and structures for their lives that worked, that made them whole and productive; *healthy,* I believe, is the word we would use today.

Because of our historical invisibility as lesbians, we are ignorant, many times, of the ways in which women who went before us *and* women in our own times have shaped their lives, coped with their difficulties, experienced their joys. A little knowledge may be a dangerous thing; but knowing there are options, knowing there have been women living as we're trying to live, is a potential defense against some of life's most gaping pitfalls.

The Women Next Door

I've chosen the nine couples described below to represent problems, issues, and delights that many lesbian couples have experienced. I've changed more than the names of each of these women, but I expect many readers to recognize these couples, these individuals. They are ourselves, our friends, our lovers. I will refer to them throughout the chapters of this book as we investigate the world of lesbian couples.

What these couples have in common, what we have in common as women who love women, are the most important things in life: falling in love, finding compatibility and intimacy, doing work that satisfies, with the support of people we love, building families or family networks that nourish us, all in the context of being allowed to be ourselves in every way.

Kathryn and Wanda became lovers on their first "real" date—within a couple of days of meeting for the first time. The chemistry between them was intense; they were both single, in their early thirties, and both had been lesbians for a long time. Neither could think of a good reason to wait for their second date. In fact, they could scarcely wait to finish dinner. "Which," Kathryn remembers, "we were having at my apartment and not in a public place, so decorum didn't matter much." Both are white women with professional lives.

Kathryn is a physical therapist with her own practice, which she worked hard to establish in a large East Coast city. As a child, she suffered from severe scoliosis and wore a brace from seventh grade through her senior year in high school. Wanda never finished college, but her skill as a fix-it handyperson was discovered by her line foreman when she worked part time at a small engine factory. Within a few years, Wanda was managing the factory's entire machinist repair crew.

The challenge facing Wanda and Kathryn today is that Wanda wants to go back to school, first to finish college—which will take only one semester—and then to go to medical school. She envies Kathryn's work with people and with healing and wants to challenge her own abilities. "I'd rather figure out what makes a person tick than rewire a soldering machine." They'll need to move to wherever Wanda is accepted at medical school, something Kathryn accepts and worries about. "I've been successful here and I think I'll be able to establish myself in another community, but it's a little scary." What is even more scary for both of them is negotiating how much Wanda is going to rely on Kathryn's income in the years ahead. "We started out as a really hot date," admits Wanda. "Now we have to see what else we're going to become."

Lisa and Mariana came out together their second year of college. Their strong racial/cultural identification—African American and Honduran—brought them together in a women's studies program that was predominantly white and heterosexual. Four years after graduation, they are still together. Lisa is an actor, struggling to make a name for herself in New York City. She earned her Equity card last year and is excited about her future. Mariana is struggling to be a writer. Both work at secretarial jobs to earn a living. They would like to have a child, or children, but their financial situation is too precarious right now, and both say they want to take their careers as far as they can. Mariana has had two articles published in an alternative-arts journal, but she is envious of Lisa's more frequent acting jobs. "It's not like I can work one weekend as an extra and get a couple of hundred dollars," she says. "I don't really mind Lisa's being able to do that, but I want it too. I got thirty dollars for an article I spent six months on." She shrugs as though it were a small thing, but it is a major problem for them, this balancing of careers.

Lisa's sharecropper family lives in rural south Texas and has no idea she is a lesbian. Mariana's parents are both dead; the grandparents who raised her live in California, and she would never tell them she is a lesbian. "They would have no idea what I was talking about," she says, laughing. "Ask my brother. He's gay and took a lover home a couple of years ago. This lover was an Anglo who was an activist in the gay movement, and he decided my brother should be out to his family. He thought he was going to have 'the big conversation' for my poor shy brother. He found out Eduardo isn't shy. You don't cause pain and confusion to your elders in my culture. Needless to say, they aren't lovers anymore. I guess that's one reason Lisa and I are so comfortable together. We respect the culture of our families."

Leslie and Daphne are proud yuppies, lipstick lesbians, they insist, who want the best of everything life has to offer. "We're DINCs [dual income no children], we just happen to be lesbian," Daphne explains casually. Both have turned thirty this year, come from white, upper-middle-class families, and went to excellent colleges. Daphne is a graphic designer with a large automotive company; Leslie is a CPA and financial planner, working with a small prestigious firm. Their combined income is over $100,000. Until the last election, they had always voted Republican. "I liked hearing Clinton talk about gays and lesbians as though we were real people, you know? It impressed me. Maybe it shouldn't have. I mean, look what's happening to all the promises." Leslie pauses and shrugs. "But I thought he ought to have a chance."

Leslie and Daphne met two years ago at a lesbian bar in Ann Arbor, where they choose to live now, although they work in Detroit. They have never joined their incomes and keep clear track of their individual expenses. Their primary commitment is to one another, but they insist their relationship is not monogamous. "It's more about how we think about ourselves," Daphne says, "whether we have other lovers or not. It keeps us from taking one another for granted." Leslie nods, "And it keeps us from fusing, you know, turning into one personality. God, so many dyke couples must bore one another to death, they're so alike in everything." In addition to not being monogamous, Leslie and Daphne are clearly identified as butch and femme when they go out to the bars. "It's another way to keep our differences more obvious." These have become very obvious in the last few months, since Leslie has begun to act on their nonmonogamy pact and is dating a woman who works as a temp in her firm.

Deborah and Peggy live in Washington, D.C., where they were both born into black middle-class families. Both are federal employees and can't imagine being out on their jobs, or to their families or communities. "Why would we want to do that?" Deborah asks comfortably. "Our private business doesn't belong out in the world." They have been living together as a couple for ten years. Deborah has a son and a daughter by different fathers. Peggy has one son. Neither has ever been married, but men—brothers, uncles, Peggy's father, and first and second cousins from both of their extended families—are in and out of the house continually. Deborah is thirty-seven and her children are nearly ready for college; Peggy is thirty-five and her son is in sixth grade.

"We're about family," Peggy says. "Sure, we like to go out to one of the bars every now and then and see some of the other girls and catch the scene, but what's important to me is our life here at home, having a good environment to raise my son, seeing that Deb's kids make it into college." They watched the gay-rights march of 1993 from a distance, viewing most of it on CNN. "Finally, Deborah said to me, 'Peggy, we're going down there.' And we did. Got down to the mall about five o'clock, and that was quite a scene." Peggy admits she is glad they went to check it out, but what seemed like a pretty snow-white scene on CNN was no less so in reality.

Peggy's hobby is weight lifting, something she's been doing with her brother since she was treated for a weak back when she was nineteen. "I don't want to ever have to lift anything heavier than a dishrag," says Deborah, laughing, "and with Peggy around, I don't have to."

Ann and Margaret met on an Olivia cruise for lesbians just a year ago. Ann was sixty-seven, white middle-class, a registered nurse living in a retirement community in the Southwest. Margaret was sixty, Jewish, from a radical working-class background, running her own tour-guide business, geared toward elderly Jewish people who want to travel comfortably. Margaret lives primarily in Mérida, Mexico. Both women are financially comfortable. Ann has a grown daughter and three grandchildren.

"I didn't think I was ever going to have another affair," Ann confesses. "I mean after my mastectomy and all, who'd want me?" She is still a little embarrassed at the intensity of the sexual attraction between these two women in their sixties, but Margaret laughs at her. "If not now, when? That's what I told her when she thought we shouldn't make love the first night out on the cruise." Margaret prevailed.

While Ann and Margaret have no intentions of living together at this time, they do see each other frequently and say they are a couple. Each has had at least one long-term marriage with another woman. What has become very clear to them in the short time they've been together is how much of their previous lives they bring to this new relationship. "I wanted to have one of those new low-water-consumption toilets put in my bathroom," Ann recounts, "and I thought I might as well redo the whole thing—tile floor, vanity, you know, decorate it nice. Margaret was visiting and she went with me to the tile factory. We couldn't agree on a single thing. I finally finished the job after she went back to Mexico."

Both women had always been the person with good taste and good ideas in their previous relationships. It never occurred to Margaret that Ann wouldn't follow her directions. "It was really frustrating," she remembers. "Here we were, six months into a relationship, having a fight about the color of a tile floor in the bathroom. I said to myself,

Maggie, remember the larger picture here and forget about the god-damned bathroom floor!" The larger picture for these two women is to see where life takes them. They both say that good health and mobility are gifts, and they don't know how long they can expect to enjoy them.

Sandra and Beth met at the local preschool in the upper-class, predominantly white neighborhood where their children were enrolled. Both were married to professional men and had given up careers to raise their children—Sandra had three and Beth four.

"My third child was born deaf," Sandra remembers, "and, while I didn't see it as a tragedy—I mean they're all *great* kids—my husband couldn't get over it. He felt guilty, or responsible, somehow. More than just the genetic roulette wheel, he felt like he'd done something wrong. It was driving us apart. And then I met Beth."

Beth is deaf. She lost most of her hearing when she had a high fever from spinal meningitis at the age of six. With hearing aids, Beth has some residual hearing, but not enough to manage without also reading lips. She can speak but prefers to sign. "I fell in love with Sandra's daughter Megan," Beth remembers. "I saw myself in her—a deaf child in a hearing world—and then I fell in love with Sandra."

After two years of intense pain and negotiations, Sandra and Beth moved in together with their seven children. Beth's lawyer husband shares custody with her, and the children spend weekends with their father. Both parents want the children to continue being active in their temple and studying Hebrew at shul. Sandra's husband vacillated between wanting to fight her for custody of the children and wanting to pretend they weren't his—no child support, nothing. "He's coming along, though, after several years of therapy. The kids spend part of the summer holidays with him at his mother's lake cottage."

Sandra and Beth were both forced to return to their careers, which has been easier in the last couple of years since their youngest child has finally started school. Everyone in their respective families knows the nature of their relationship. "How could we hide something so complicated?" Beth asks. But neither is out at work. Beth is a legal secretary in a large law firm, and Sandra teaches kindergarten. At thirty-five and thirty-six, they feel their life is beginning to settle into something that feels normal to them, however chaotic it may look from the outside.

When Barbara and Susan met at a NOW meeting in a rural community in southern Illinois, only Barbara thought she was a lesbian. Long divorced, raising her nine-year-old daughter on her own, Barbara was enjoying life as a single lesbian. She loved dancing and flirting. Susan was married and trying to conceive a child with her husband. "That was before I went dancing with Barbara," she admits. "I said to myself, What's the harm? I can go once, right?" She did. Three months later she left her husband. Within a year she was living with Barbara and had conceived a child from an anonymous donor in the gay male community.

Both are white, working-class women. After several years of struggling with dead-end, low-paying jobs, Barbara and Susan began their own construction business. "That makes it sound grander than it is," Barbara corrects Susan. "What we've been is carpenters who will attempt almost anything. And you'd be amazed at how many people are more comfortable having us around than a man. Not just dykes, but people who need a job done while they're away at work, that kind of thing."

When Susan's son was eight, settled in school, and Barbara's daughter left for college, just when they thought they'd have more time for one another, Barbara was diagnosed with ovarian cancer. Surgery showed it to be quite advanced. Chemotherapy slowed but didn't stop it. Now they count time in days and weeks instead of years.

Sarah and Joline met when they were girls. Although they were three years apart in age, they became close friends, and early on their families got used to the fact that Sarah and Jo were inseparable. Sometime during the year when Sarah was sixteen and Jo thirteen, they became lovers. Now, twenty years later, they can't remember exactly how it happened, and they certainly didn't name the sex, themselves, or their relationship as lesbian. But something shifted and they knew they were different, that they had a secret. Jo's father is a Baptist minister in one of the largest black congregations in their city. Sarah's family is white working class. Because they had no way to name themselves, they lived with that secret for fifteen years, while Joline went to nursing school and Sarah began work as a grocery-store clerk.

But when Sarah and Jo were in their late twenties, they began to realize there were other women, living together as couples, whose lives seemed to resemble theirs. Gradually, they began to talk with one another about what they were living, and eventually they talked to one or two of those other women who seemed so familiar. Sarah was a store manager now and saw younger women working for her who wore their hair short and made no effort to hide what they were. Jo took a call on her floor at the hospital for another nurse—"Tell her to call home," said the woman on the line, and the message came through to Jo loud and clear. When she was thirty, Jo went into counseling, briefly, with a lesbian therapist and began to discover an even wider world.

By the time Sarah and Jo celebrated their twentieth anniversary (at the ages of thirty-three and thirty-six!), they were able to do so with a dozen friends who were lesbian couples like themselves. Today Jo's three sisters know that Sarah and Jo call themselves lesbians, but they've chosen not to tell anyone else in the families because of their circumstances—Jo's father, she says, couldn't accept it and she doesn't want to give him pain. Sarah has never felt any need to name her relationship with Jo to her family. "It just is what it is," she says. "They've been used to me being with Jo forever. It's a fact of life."

Joan and Marty are in their late forties. They met when they were thirty-one, both the same age, both ardent feminists in the new and exciting feminist movement of the seventies. Both were white middle class, but their differences seemed more important to them at the time. Marty, a teacher, had been a nun for twelve years, until the fading promise of Vatican II had led her to seek a "fulfilled life" outside the Church. She had come out of the convent and come out as a lesbian in the same moment. Joan was a high-powered salesperson for a large computer company and had just recently "come out" with a woman who was no longer a part of her life, a fact she was still mourning.

Joan and Marty met at a feminist conference, where each was circumspectly exploring her newly established identity. Within a few months Joan had left her job in New York City and moved to the country, where Marty had found a teaching position. For these women, living in the country didn't mean hiding. They began a lesbian support group and started a lesbian-only bed-and-breakfast for women visiting the nearby summer tourist attractions. They made a lot of their life decisions based on what they called their "politics."

Both of their families know they are lesbians, and while these conversations weren't easy, neither of them was disowned by her family. They investigated the possibility of adopting a child and discussed having a child by artificial insemination, but by then the relationship seemed tenuous and they didn't follow through. The fact that Marty lost her job as a result of being so out in their community may also have contributed to their decision not to have a child. After seventeen years together, the last seven filled with struggle and heartache for both of them, they recently separated. Today they admit that their alcohol use/abuse was a major factor in destroying the relationship.

The discussions about and examples from these women's lives and my own life are not an attempt to codify behavior or create rules for how to be lesbians or how to be lesbian couples. My concern is to examine how lesbians are coming together as couples, what our special challenges are, and what some of us have done about them. We can raise our awareness by raising the issues. Once that's done, we'll each have to find the solutions we are comfortable with.

REFERENCES

1. Lillian Faderman, *Surpassing the Love of Men: Romantic Friendship and Love Between Women from the Renaissance to the Present*. New York: William Morrow, 1981.

2. Carroll Smith-Rosenberg, "The Female World of Love and Ritual: Relations Between Women in Nineteenth-Century America," *Signs: Journal of Women in Culture and Society*, Vol. I, no. 1, Autumn, 1975, pp. 1–29.

3. Judith C. Brown, "Lesbian Sexuality in Renaissance Italy: The Case of Sister Benedetta Carlini," *Signs*, Vol. IX, no. 4, pp. 751–58.

4. John Boswell, *Christianity, Social Tolerance, and Homosexuality*. Chicago: University of Chicago Press, 1980, p. 290.

5. Brown, p. 757.

6. Smith-Rosenberg, p. 1.

PART TWO

Lesbians and Sex

Is *She* a Lesbian?

Radar. That's how we tell. Dykes have built-in scanners, sort of like twenty-four-hour radar stations that rotate inside our skulls. We always know another lesbian. We can tell by her vibes, right? Myth #1. We wish.

Her haircut. A clear indicator, you say? The short dyke-do. Or maybe the "come over to my house and I'll give you a trim" cut.

The labyris hanging out of her shirt front.

The dyke walk. The dyke look. There is definitely a "look," my twenty-something informants assure me. "Like," says one, "if I was walking down the street and gave you the look, you'd know." Uh-huh. Like I'd know?

If all else fails? You check her haircut, her look, and you still can't tell? Consult the grapevine. It's infallible. If you can find it.

If sexuality were a fixed thing, it might be easier, this question of is she or isn't she. But the woman who was straight today could be gay tomorrow, and it even works the other way around, though we'd prefer to ignore that.

Furthermore, in my generation, women didn't expect to grow up and be the initiator in these matters. We expected to wait and be asked. That's a big mistake, if you're waiting for another woman to ask. When I was coming out, my fantasy life was basically about being seduced by a fabulous, beautiful, skilled woman who would let me be the passive observer of my own seduction. I could have waited a long time, believe me, for that to happen. Fortunately, I'm impatient. I asked, she said yes.

I knew she was a lesbian because she'd said it out loud. That was very helpful. For at least two years before that, I'd been falling in love with women who *might* have been lesbians, but were, in fact, straight—not an uncommon detour, I've found, for lesbians who want to come out. She knew I was a lesbian (even if I hadn't officially crossed the line by making love with a woman) because I told her I was.

"How did I know Kathryn was a lesbian?" asks Wanda, the machinist who wants to go to medical school. "What else would she be? I met her at the dyke bar. She was with friends. I was with friends. We danced quite a while and then I gave her my phone number." She shrugs, as if this is an everyday occurrence.

Have you ever wondered about a woman, I ask her, really been attracted but not sure? "Maybe," she concedes, "way back when I first came out." She's acting like it's hard to remember that far back. "But since then my friends are mostly lesbians, I go to a lot of lesbian events. I figure any woman I meet in the places where I'm hanging out is probably a lesbian." She laughs. "Or she wants to be."

Sandra and Beth—the married middle-class housewives—are just three years older than Wanda and Kathryn, but their experience is totally different. Each married early, had children, and then fell in love with one another. "Did I know she was a lesbian?" Sandra laughs. "No. I knew she wasn't. At least if you looked at our lives, neither was I. I wasn't attracted to her because she was a lesbian, it was—I don't know just what it was, actually." She pauses, thoughtful.

"I was pretty sure what was happening from the start," Beth admits quietly. "I'd been attracted to another woman a few years before. Nothing real serious, but I made a mental note of it. When I met Sandra, something inside me said, Uh-oh. I mean I had real warning signals going off." But instead of paying negative attention to whatever signals she was picking up, Beth was thrilled. "I love feeling intensely. About everything, really. But with Sandra, well, my nerves were singing. I knew this was going to be major. And I knew she'd feel it too. If not at first, then soon."

Beth and Sandra only know one or two other lesbians. Most of their lives focus around their children, their work. They don't assume the women they are friendly with will be lesbians, because for the most part they aren't. But when it came to knowing one another, the radar really did work.

What Will We Be? Friends, Lovers, Partners?

I've done it. Haven't we all? She's a friend. It seems like it would be a lot easier to turn her into a lover than to go out and look for another woman who could be a friend and lover. But it didn't work, it doesn't work. For many reasons, my friends are my friends, not my lovers. Because we love one another but aren't sexually attracted; because we love one another and might have been sexually attracted at one time, but she (or I) was already involved and it would have been messy; because I can put up with her quirks and foibles as a friend when I spend only a few hours a day with her, but the thought of coming home to her would make me crazy (or make her crazy); or just because we are too much alike and our strengths don't complement and support one another's weaknesses.

Then there's that horrible moment that has probably occurred at least once to each of us—when you've realized that what you thought was a date, with real lover possibilities, was only happening in *your* head, to *your* hormones. She is blithely unaware of your turmoil. The kiss she gives you after the intense conversation over dinner, after the warm connection during the play, was a sisterly kiss. Her hug is enthusiastic, but that kiss is definitely not testing the waters, so to speak. And you were ready to start fingering the buttons on her blouse.

Women have told me that sexual attraction *can't* happen to one person, that the other woman must be involved, even if she's denying it, because we just don't get there by ourselves. If Myth #1 is that we can *always* tell another lesbian, this is Myth #2—that passion begets passion. My experience tells me otherwise, but it's not exactly an issue we can get a grant to study scientifically, so it will probably always be something we can disagree about. My first lover told me I was fairly stupid about recognizing when a woman was attracted to me, which she saw as a serious failing to take responsibility in relationships. Since then I've learned I don't need to take responsibility for another person's feelings; it's quite honorable enough to be responsible for mine. And I've learned it is true that I don't always pay as much attention as I might to what is developing in a relationship.

When we are lucky, in a "best case" scenario, both women know what they want as the relationship develops, and both women want the same thing, at the same time.

Sarah and Joline's relationship grew in the same way, and they both seemed to have moved at the same pace. They went from being best childhood friends to being best lovers, and it's lasted for twenty years. But it's hard to judge. Was that sexual spark always there? Joline can't remember. She always remembers loving Sarah, from the first day she met her on the school playground. "Sarah was older and she looked after me, at first. Then we got to be buddies—the Mutt and Jeff of the playground scene. She was this tall blonde white girl and there was short, dumpy little me. I did grow up to her size after a while. Maybe that's when it changed."

Sarah remembers there being a lot of tension at the turning point in their relationship, but she couldn't have named it as sexual tension. "I was sixteen and I knew I was doing something I wasn't supposed to. But that feeling could have been connected to race as easily as to sex. Ask me if I'm attracted to Jo today and I can answer you."

The answer is yes, of course. For Sarah and Jo, the chemistry was there long before they could name it.

I wondered if it was easier at the other end of the spectrum, after some experience in the world. Is it more obvious then, whether we're courting a friend or a lover/friend? I asked Ann, the oldest lesbian in this sample group, if, when she went over to sit down next to Margaret on the first day of the Olivia cruise, she was looking for a lover or for someone to be a "pal" for the duration of the cruise. "A friend," she said without hesitation. "If I'd thought it was about anything else, I wouldn't have had the nerve to approach her."

Margaret laughs at this, but, watching Ann's face, one feels she is probably telling the truth. Margaret took the initiative after that, changing her dining-room time so that she could sit with Ann. By lunchtime, they both knew sex was a possibility. "I could tell because I was getting tense," Ann remembers. "I hadn't had a lover since my mastectomy three years ago and I started wondering how I should tell her that I only had one breast. That was when I knew."

Usually we do know, whether it's sooner or later. Confusion? I suspect that means we are wishing for something that isn't there.

Just as men and women who are heterosexual have to find their ways around the boundaries of sex if they are going to be friends instead of lovers, so do two women who are lesbians. You're attracted to a woman who is happily involved with a long-term lover? You feel "come fly with me" vibes from an exciting new acquaintance, and you have no intention of leaving your current lover or experimenting with nonmonogamy? What's a dyke to do?

Enjoy. Sexual tension *can* be a gift, if we think of it that way. It means we are alive, vibrant, aware, sexual. It does not mean we have to act on those feelings with the person who stimulated them. It does not mean we are being "mentally" unfaithful, or somehow bad. In fact, I have had sexual feeling toward most of the lesbians who are today my best and closest friends, and I have not acted on—or wanted to act on—those feelings or felt trapped or diminished by them. They go with the territory, these feelings. The trick is to acknowledge them and the circumstances that surround them. If either or both of you can't or doesn't want to act on those sexual promptings, let it be. But if she's available, and you're available, go for it!

When I was forty-seven, I met the woman who is my lover today. After just a few days of learning who she was, it became very clear to me that there was no way I wanted this woman to be only my friend, no way. I felt about seventeen again, my hormones were raging, my pulse did impossible things when she walked into my house. I hadn't responded to anyone like this in years; in fact, I thought I wouldn't ever again. I thought I had learned that the best way to approach a relationship is to let it grow slowly, test the waters, make sure where you each are emotionally, decide in a calm manner whether to let this grow and develop. Wrong. My heart/hormones took a deep plunge off the high dive, and all I could do was hope the water was deep enough so I didn't crash-land. And hope that she felt in some measure the way I did. There's nothing worse than being on the high dive all by yourself.

Well, it wasn't exactly that impulsive. I did keep looking around me. I wanted to know her history—not from the safe-sex perspective. I wanted to know how she had treated her other lovers, how they became ex-lovers, where they were in her life today. Generally, I liked what I learned, and some of that learning, I think, allowed me to relax and let my hormones take over. But it never occurred to me that this relationship was about finding a new friend or a buddy; this one included sex from the start.

I have been told, unequivocally, that lesbians don't date. Myth #3. Dating is something heterosexuals do in high school. Lesbians "see somebody" or "get involved" or "spend quality time together." Really! Will we do anything to avoid the d-word? Anyway, we can't do what they do on dates, like hold hands in the movies or walk through the park with stars in our eyes and our arms around each other, can we? Well, some of us have and more of us will; so let's abandon the myth that lesbians don't date.

Right. What is a date anyhow?

Dating is a variety of things. A date is a way of testing the waters, whether or not we ever want to take the plunge. It can be that ritual dance we do before commitment—or a ritual we use because we're not looking for commitment. It may include sex or the exploration of sexual energy, however that occurs, but it is definitely different from going to the movies with a buddy.

So how do we date? One friend tells me she waits to be asked. Another says she lets the woman she's interested in know through the grapevine that she's interested—like, tell Sarah and hope that Sarah will tell Susan that Jean is interested in "seeing" Susan and that Susan will have enough wit or enough contacts to both get the message and make a move. In one part of the country, I'm told, you can't do anything without first going for coffee. Nope, not even a movie. In other places the movie comes first, then you have coffee and talk about *it*. We call these rituals, culturally defined, geographically specific; nonetheless, they are rituals. As dates are rituals.

For some of us, it's been so long since we did anything resembling "dating" that the ritual seems more foreign than familiar. Sandra and Beth, the couple with seven children between them, agree that dating was not exactly how they'd describe their coming together. They'd drop kids off at day care, pretend to be surprised to see one another, and make an elaborate charade of "spontaneously" going for coffee. And yet, Sandra admits, "I counted on that time with her all weekend. Monday morning my husband would go back to work, the older two kids would take the bus to school, and I'd bundle Megan into her car seat, humming with excitement because I knew I was going to see *her*." The excitement was mutual. "Nothing," Beth agreed, "would keep me from taking Rachel and David to day care. I don't think we missed one Monday morning during the whole year."

Mondays were important because then they'd arrange their schedule for the rest of the week, never meeting fewer than three times a week. Sandra had been learning sign language since the day she had found out her daughter Megan was deaf, and practicing sign language was as good an excuse as any for these meetings. "After two or three months," says Beth, "I knew it was about sex. I just didn't know if *she* knew, and I didn't know how we were going to figure out how to do anything about it if she *did* know."

How did they do it? Bring up the forbidden topic of sex? "I'm not very patient," admits Beth. "Maybe it's connected to being deaf and not wanting to miss anything. Maybe it's just my personality. But I did it." Did what? "Told her I wanted to make love to her." Beth laughs. "I told her over coffee in a public place so she wouldn't think I was about to jump her, and I hoped she'd sit still long enough to hear me out." And what happened? "She jumped me. Well, almost." Beth is grinning at the memory and Sandra is silently shaking her head. "Yes, you did," insists Beth. "We left the café in about ten seconds and headed for her house, where no one was home."

It can be tough, those first hours, days, weeks, when you aren't really sure what she means, sometimes not even what you mean. I've told a woman, in words or gestures, that I wanted to make love to her and seen her look of surprise as she responded, "Oh, that isn't what I meant at all." I might have been disappointed, but I wasn't devastated, and at least the confusion was gone. Knowing is easier on a relationship than not knowing, and I highly recommend asking—in one way or another.

In a very real sense, Sandra and Beth were dating during that beginning time when they were having coffee together on Monday mornings. Not quite as obviously as Leslie and Daphne, who met at a gay bar and exchanged phone numbers, but dating. "Of course lesbians date," Leslie says, laughing, "if by dating you mean having sex with someone and not being sure you want to have anything else with her. I mean, not like moving in together on the second date and all that, but dating. Playing the field. All those things men do that we're not supposed to." Leslie prides herself on being fairly "out there" sexually. When she was single, she asked women out frequently, and says they never doubted the sexual nature of her invitation. She asked women for dates whenever she saw a woman she found interesting, exciting. "I didn't get too concerned about figuring out whether they were lesbians or not. If they weren't, they could say no. Usually, though, the women I'd ask out were giving me some signs of interest. And if something starts developing, why should I care what she calls herself?"

I watched Leslie at a basketball game one night several years ago, before she was with Daphne. She saw a woman three rows back she was interested in. For the first half of the game, she looked back, paid obvious attention to the woman, who began to notice Leslie's attention. At half time, Leslie went up to her row and managed to talk with this woman. "So?" I asked her when she came back to her seat for the second half. She shrugged and smiled. At the end of the game, as we were filing out of the stadium, the woman was waiting for us at the top of the stairs. She handed something to Leslie, smiled shyly, then walked away with her friends. "Yes," said Leslie grinning. She showed me a matchbook with a phone number and first name written on it.

I was never as "out there" as Leslie, but after my first long-term relationship ended, I spent eight years as a single lesbian, and I learned something about these dating rituals firsthand. I've invited women to dinner and hoped it would be more than dinner. I've gone to concerts and plays and films. I've accepted invitations, too— "Come over for dinner, we want you to meet our friend Jane." Uh-huh. One woman and I spent most of the fall taking vigorous walks through the city between 10 P.M. and midnight. When she invited me to spend a weekend at a friend's country house, I assumed I was on a date. I was right, but the chemistry between us never developed. I found out later she was seeing another woman at the same time and trying to make some choices. Obviously, I wasn't the choice.

What I learned for myself was that the titillation of not knowing for sure what was happening only lasted a short while. After that, if it hadn't become plain, I wanted to know what was going on. Is this a date or are we just hanging out here? In the instances when I was clearly interested and the other woman wasn't, my libido diminished fairly rapidly. I wasn't someone who could wait and keep my interest at a fever pitch.

Some women have told me just the opposite, that their most intense pleasure comes in the ritualized dance of advance/retreat, advance/retreat. Leslie, for example, enjoys being pursued, on occasion, by an aggressive femme. "But she has to play the game, you know? Back off and let me make a move. I don't like being hit on. And I want a woman who's interested, not one who's needy. To me, dating's a game and if you don't play it that way, what's the point?"

I personally never saw dating as a game. I was too worried about figuring out what I was feeling, letting the other person know what I was feeling, and listening to find out what she was feeling. I'd like to have been able to relax more, but it isn't me. Leslie says that the game *can* get serious. She met Daphne on a date, and after a few months of intense playing, they decided to live together. "We still flirt," Daphne hastens to add. "We're very playful together, that's one of the things that drew us together. But we have made a commitment to one another."

Neither Leslie nor I was "right" in how we dated, but on a date together we would have been a disaster. She would have been playing and I would have been taking her seriously. When she whispered an exaggerated sweet nothing as she nibbled on my ear, I'm afraid I would have fled in a panic because she was moving too fast, getting serious too soon.

So whatever we call it, lesbians do date. I don't know whether we date more or less than straight women or gay men. I suspect dating is an age-related practice. A friend confessed recently that her twenty-year-old daughter had seen six boyfriends in the last four months. She gave each of them about two weeks, then moved on. I don't think that's very different from the patterns I've seen in younger lesbians—they're exploring sexually, but have lots of other things they need to pay attention to, like work or school, figuring out how to support themselves. Settling down with a chosen mate isn't high on the immediacy list.

Lesbians with careers, with children, with well-established lives, may focus more on finding that one woman. I did. When I came out as a lesbian in my early thirties, I was involved briefly with two women and then met the woman who was to be my lover for eight years. We became lovers in October, she moved into my apartment in January, and the following year we bought a house together. It never occurred to me that I wouldn't be coupled. Gay men might have multiple relationships, brag about the number of anonymous sexual partners they were with on a vacation in San Francisco (this was the safe seventies), but lesbians, I was sure, lived together in couples. At least the ones I knew did.

Today, dating patterns among lesbians and gay men are changing. I don't know a single gay man anymore who brags about anonymous sexual encounters, but I do know a lesbian who does. And I know gay men who are looking desperately for that one man to settle down with, a response to AIDS, surely, but also to a different kind of longing, something that went unperceived during the hectic years of post-Stonewall and pre-HIV.

In my experience, which has been primarily with women of my generation, lesbians have a hard time being casual about our relationships. Many of us seem to have a built-in homing device, which drones at a subconscious level: "Grab her and settle down, grab her and settle down." A friend says it happened to her. She wasn't thinking consciously about living with anyone, but she dated a woman a couple of times, and then it seemed easier to just let it go along developing. "I let it develop," she remembers, "in spite of knowing that this woman didn't suit me very well, that we weren't much of a match. But letting her move in was easier, I guess, than dealing with ending it or telling her I'd rather be friends. And at some level it was what both of us expected—after the second date." But why? I push her for more answers. "Lesbians have to break through one level of gender expectations, you know, that the woman is passive, just to become lovers. And then there's the stuff about its being taboo, forbidden. In my generation"—she is in her late forties—"that about exhausts my adrenaline rush after I notice I'm attracted to someone. Taking more initiative?" She shakes her head. "It's too hard."

During the eight years I considered myself a "single and dating" lesbian, the "making a home" impulse surfaced to consciousness whenever I was seeing someone for more than a week. I *had* created one circumstance that helped me, however. When my first long-term relationship ended, I knew I needed to be alone, probably for more than a few months, while I figured out my life. I decided that, as a mode of self-preservation, I had better live in a space that was only large enough for one.

Women who walked into my space recognized that I was living alone. I hoped they would also recognize that I liked living alone, because my space suited me. It fit like my favorite pair of jogging sweats. Living alone was a statement that I didn't need someone to complete me. Making that statement was necessary because of the voices in my head telling me it was "normal" or "better" to be coupled.

"Sure, I've heard those voices," admits Leslie. "And so have a fair share of the women I've dated. I can't tell you how often a second date is taken as an invitation to permanence." She shrugs it off as just one of those things you have to expect. "I just wasn't interested until I met Daphne." Being coupled, however, wasn't something Daphne could take or leave. "I like knowing what I can count on." For Daphne, that meant a kind of serial monogamy, dating one woman exclusively, leaving her when she wanted to start seeing someone else.

Since college, Daphne has been involved with five women and lived with three of them. Her first lover, after she moved out of the college dorm and out to Detroit to begin her job as a graphic designer with an auto company, was a woman in her department. "We were talking about being roommates before we became lovers. It just seemed natural, since decent housing was so outrageous, for two single women to talk about living together." They became lovers while they were apartment hunting and lived together for nearly a year.

"That was about my average until I met Leslie," Daphne confesses. "When June, my first lover, started seeing someone else, I went a little crazy. I went out to the bars to get picked up. I only did it once, that time." She's laughing now. "Sheila, the woman who took me home, invited me to stay. So I did. We had great sex that night and the next morning I said I'd see her that evening, and by the next weekend most of my clothes were at her place anyway."

Why? I asked Daphne. Why so little time for reflection, for seeing what might have been right or wrong about the relationship she'd just left? Isn't that one of the benefits of dating, however much we hate the word?

She understands the question and answers slowly. "I guess I thought that the new relationship would make right anything that was wrong with the last one. I know better than that today," she adds hastily. "But in my twenties . . . " She left that dangling as though it were self-evident, but I have known many women in their twenties who were able to reflect on the quality of their relationships and decide what was working for them, what wasn't, and what they really wanted in a partner.

"It's like this," twenty-six-year-old Lisa, the actor, explains patiently to me. "Just going out with someone, hanging out with them and sleeping with them, that's a lot easier than meeting someone and developing a friendship and wanting the friendship to grow into a lover relationship. In the latter case, you have to think about what you're doing. . . ." She pauses, frowning. "That's hard work. It's what Mariana and I did, but there were a lot of young dykes around us in college who were sleeping with anyone who was willing." "Yeah," Mariana interjects, "and sometimes they'd even surprise themselves by sleeping with someone they really liked, and then they'd start trying to develop a relationship. There's nothing wrong with doing it that way, really. It just isn't how we did it."

Barbara and Susan see it differently from their rural perspective. "You've heard the joke about what lesbians do on the second date?" Barbara asks. "Rent a Hertz truck and move in together?" I have. I imagine we all have. "We may joke about it, but for a lot of lesbians, we've never really done anything but meet somebody and decide right away: this is who I'm going to be with for a while. So there's not a lot of time between the initial meeting and commitment. There's no time to look around and see if this is what I want. I did that with every relationship before I met Susan. Even if they only lasted a couple of months, basically we were living together after the second date. I guess the reason it was a little different with Susan was that she was married and couldn't move in until after her divorce!"

"Right," Susan agrees, "and even then I wasn't in a hurry to move in, but Dave wanted me out and that was hard to disagree with, given the circumstances."

"I don't really see what's wrong with it." Barbara smiles, remembering. "It's that way with dykes all over the world. You meet someone, you're physically attracted, and you take a vacation from your life for a few days or weeks. You don't have to get out of bed except to pee. You don't need to sleep because you're too busy making love or talking. And I think that's so wonderful. We ask, Why do lesbians do this? and maybe the question is, Why not?"

The why not is that too many lesbians have told me they've ended up in relationships they didn't want or shouldn't have been involved in, but the possibility was there and they just kept on wandering down that road. The getting in was easy, but getting out was horrendous and hurtful. Even with my apartment that would only fit one, I had my share of hard experiences during the eight years I was single.

One of the things I knew I wanted, after several false starts, was a lover who shared my love of the outdoors, my enthusiasm for jogging, hiking, camping. Other women might go on exotic vacations at resort hotels or on cruises, but my real longing was for a woman who'd share my tent. I let myself recognize that desire, and when I met my present lover, it was one of my dreams that came true. Not the first thing I asked her, mind you, and not the thing that would have prevented me from loving her if she hadn't wanted to share my tent. But when she said she loved to hike and camp and we began to compare mountains we had climbed or wanted to climb, my comfort level with this relationship slid up an extra notch.

On the reverse side, a number of lesbians I know are having or adopting children. Right now, for my life, I know I don't want to raise a child, especially not a young one. I want to write books and be free to travel. When a woman I was seeing announced she wanted a child and was ready to begin the process of artificial insemination, I knew it was the end of our potential to be partners. That knowing was painful, but it was certainly preferable to "realizing" several years into a child's life that I was a resentful and unhappy coparent.

Looking at a relationship, assessing it and discovering that it isn't what I want for my life, requires a consciousness that is sometimes painful and can occasionally seem cruel. Inevitably, it is less difficult when the assessment is made before the commitment rather than after. That doesn't mean lesbians should stop falling in love with one another at first sight—or taste—there's not a chance of that. But it does mean we should be thinking about what we want for our lives during those times when we aren't head over heels.

Lesbian Passion

The media is just discovering us. There are lesbians on talk shows, on the cover of *Newsweek*, and in a review of six new erotica anthologies of stories from a woman's perspective, Lennard J. Davis discovers that, "based on the fantasies of these works, we can now answer Freud's question, 'What do women want?' definitively—they want cunnilingus."[1] I don't know if he counted, but Davis goes on to say that there are hundreds of descriptions of oral sex in these works and that, in addition to tongues, "fingers play major roles." This might be expected if he were reviewing six books of lesbian erotica, but none of these books is exclusively about lesbians. In fact, one is about sex between married heterosexuals, another is an anthology of African American erotica. Given this context, what Davis is actually surprised about here is the virtual absence of the penis, not only as the centerpiece of the erotic experience, but even as a peripheral player.

> New metaphors and adjectives jump into the narrative flow of pornography as the old clichés about size and hardness yield to a poetics of wet and small. All this reminds us that sex is not just what comes naturally but is more about how society constructs the body. New generations will find here analogues to their own shapes of desire.[2]

We hope there *will* be new shapes of desire, constructed by new generations of women, especially. As a culture we need to be turned on by passionate sex and turned off by the fantasies of rape and physical brutality that currently pass for "sex." Our culture *does* decide what is beautiful, romantic, erotic. The ideal of female beauty today resembles the body of an adolescent male, small-breasted and long-limbed. Rubenesque is out. *Zaftig* is a derogatory term. To some extent, I have seen this image change in my lifetime, in my own idea of what is beautiful. When I look at photographs of Marilyn Monroe today—and she was the erotic ideal of my growing-up years—she looks overweight to me. I don't like that, but it's true.

Just as our idea of what is beautiful can be created or manipulated, our sexual appetites—the desire out of which passion or lust flows—can also be constructed. And they can be manipulated—by the media, by a lover, by ourselves. As a writer, I have struggled with the language of sex, of sexuality. When I was writing a lesbian romance, *Just Say Yes*,[3] I wanted to create sex scenes that would be a "turn-on." It wasn't easy, but learning how to do it was fun and the research was great. What I found was that I had to construct a scene that would have some tension even without the sex, because sex all by itself is just sex. It isn't automatically erotic.

I discovered this by reading other sexual descriptions, gay and straight, literary and pornographic. Occasionally, a passage would arouse me because of its lyrical beauty, like the scene between Cholly and Pauline in Toni Morrison's *The Bluest Eye*,[4] a description that I consider one of the finest I've ever read of hetero sex. Others were so badly written that I'd start laughing hysterically. So much for both arousal and research. Gradually, I began to notice a trend, however, and at first I didn't know whether to deplore or utilize it. Scenes of sex in public, with the threat of exposure, and scenes in which there was a voluntary power differential seemed more exciting to me than "jogger with great breasts happens on sweaty mower-of-lawn with great biceps," and they fuck happily with no introductions and no consequences in real life.

I did use what I learned in my research and created a sex scene on the pier in Provincetown that has received rave reviews from various sources other than my best friends, and I created another "play" scene in which the participants chose to be dominant and submissive. But the challenge came when I wanted to write a sexual "love scene" between two women who were contemplating making a commitment to one another. Without props, I had to create the tension in the scene through the language of sexual lust born of love and the urgency of fulfilling that desire.

As lesbians, we may wish that our sexual desires—that most private part of who we are, which we share with only a few intimates—were ours and ours alone, unaffected by the culture at large, unaffected by the images of violence and woman-hating surrounding us in the mainstream culture. But it isn't so. It can't be. None of us is cut off enough from books, television, movies, and the ubiquitous news broadcast to be unaffected by these images. Some of us, indeed, are the victims on which these images are based. But I maintain that it is not only the rape survivors, the incest survivors, the battered women who are affected. Images of violence in our culture tend to be a bit like the chlorine in our water system. We all notice the smell, the taste, at first, but after a while it is what we know, what we are used to, and we forget to complain.

In addition, it is rare that lesbians ever see our own lust or passion reflected back to us in films, books, television. We are inundated with images of heterosexual sexuality. The occasional lesbian we do encounter in the media is a twisted, psychotic killer, or a male heterosexual's pornographic fantasy.

So passion is tricky. It's not entirely ours to create; and yet we aren't totally at the mercy of our unconscious—that gremlin whispering secret messages to our brain and libido. If passion were only about what the mainstream culture funnels to us through the mass media, two middle-aged women would never be found lusting after one another. And we know that happens, probably more often than anyone thinks.

Lesbians are trying to create a new consciousness about sex, sexuality, passion, and desire. Some of us advocate censoring the old, harmful images of violent pornography. Others say we should ignore the old and get on with making our own. The one thing I believe for myself about all of this is that censorship is a waste of time because it doesn't work. It doesn't change consciousness and it does inhibit conversations and education that can change consciousness. If censorship were effective, the fifty-year ban on anti-Semitic expressions in the Soviet Union and Eastern Europe ought to have eradicated the anti-Semitic impulse. In the last few years, as the ban has been lifted because the official state censoring apparatus was weakening, it became horrifyingly obvious that anti-Semitic feeling had only festered, unchanged, under the clamped-down lid of censorship.

Personally, I'm not going to try to censor anyone else's expression. I can refuse to support work that threatens or offends me, boycott films, not buy certain magazines. But my choice for now is to concentrate on creating the new and phasing the old into oblivion. Lesbian sex. It may be newly fashionable, but it's as old as time and there are hundreds of ways to do it.

Sex for the First Time—with a New Lover

She came for dinner, but we both knew it was about sex. For the first time. I scrubbed my house down with once-a-year thoroughness. I was too nervous to sit at my computer and work. Might as well do something useful. I showered. I changed clothes three times. Only shorts and a T-shirt, because it was late May and warm, but I couldn't decide on which shorts and which T-shirt. Finally, she arrived. A quick hug at the door. A cup of coffee while I finished making dinner. She was setting the table when we bumped into one another in the middle of my small kitchen. A kiss. A longer kiss. A very long, deep kiss. I tasted her, inhaled her. When we broke for a moment to breathe, she said, "I guess I'd better bring in my clothes for work tomorrow. I left them in the car." Smart woman.

"Oh, good," I agreed. And thought, thank God. The uncertainty was over. However awkward the rest of the "firsts" might be, at least now we both knew what we were about.

Getting to that place happens differently each time. But the basic elements are the same. We're drawn to someone. We wonder. We negotiate. We're tense with nervous energy and hope she is feeling it too. Finally, one of us moves directly forward, over the line of uncertainty. Or we both move toward it at the same moment. Today, I can't remember who initiated the kiss in the kitchen. It doesn't matter. But it had to happen so that we could go forward.

Barbara drove Susan home from their first dance date and dropped her off at her husband's house. "It felt kind of weird to me," Barbara confesses, "like I was a teenager again and I was taking her back to her father's or something." The second date each drove her own car and they met at the bar, now that Susan knew where it was. "We started making out during one of the slow dances," Susan remembers. "I thought I would faint. I mean, I'd had sex with my husband and a couple of other men, but I never felt anything like I did that night. She had me so turned on she could have done anything she wanted to me, right there on the dance floor." And then they left the bar and they had two cars and Susan's husband was waiting for her, so she drove home alone.

"The third time, we figured it out." Barbara laughs. "She drove to my house and we did actually get in my car to drive to the bar, but we never got out of the driveway." Within a few minutes they were back inside and in Barbara's bedroom. Barbara, having had no doubt about Susan's desires since their first date, had made arrangements to have her daughter sleep over at a friend's house that night. "It was awesome," Susan remembers fondly. "By the time I drove home, I *knew* I wanted a divorce."

Was it more awkward, I wondered, since Susan had never made love with a woman before? "No, goddess, no. I'd been thinking about it, fantasizing about it, dreaming about it for months." She's laughing now. "The only thing that felt awkward was how anxious I was to take her clothes off. And she was holding back, because she was still seeing me as a married woman." Ah, yes, the things we tell ourselves we'll never do. I will never no never make love to a straight woman. I will never make love to a woman x years younger than me. I asked Barbara what changed her mind. "About halfway through the undressing, I realized this was no straight woman. I'd had sex with a couple of women who were, you know, experimenting. And the deal was they wanted me to make love to them, but they weren't very interested in my body. Susan was interested. What can I say?"

All of the women I talked with agreed that difference in levels of sexual expertise was seldom a problem. "We're quick learners, I guess," Barbara said, laughing. What was perceived as a problem was a scenario in which two women made love, became lovers, then monogamous partners, when one of them had been with different women and one of them was being with a woman for the first time. "She should experiment," insists Leslie. "How can she possibly know what will suit her best if she's only been with one woman?"

Beth and Sandra disagree. Neither had ever been with a woman before they became lovers and they insist they have no urge to experiment further. "Getting this far was hard enough," says Sandra. "We didn't do this as an experiment. This is our life." They agree that making love for the first time was a little awkward, but nothing they couldn't manage. "Experience is relative," Sandra said, smiling. "I'd imagined making love to her for so long I knew exactly what I wanted to do."

First times can, on occasion, be difficult negotiations, no matter how experienced the women involved are. Ann and Margaret were on a cruise ship, surrounded by dykes, and suggestions of sex were everywhere. "By midafternoon," Ann confesses,"I was sure I wanted no part of this. I didn't want to have to deal with her seeing my mastectomy scar. I've got three spare tires around my middle now, not one, and I just didn't want to have to deal."

What happened? "I could see she was uneasy," Margaret says. "She was withdrawing and that was the last thing I wanted, so I backed off. I'd rather have had a friendship than nothing at all. I didn't want to be alone for the whole two weeks on this cruise ship either, so what the hell." I ask again, So what happened? Margaret, apparently, started talking about her life, her dreams, her disappointments. She told Ann about her twenty-five-year relationship with her life partner, Rachel, and her devastation at Rachel's death in a commercial airplane crash seven years before. "We were mates, mated, in every sense of the word. Like a pair of cardinals, where if one is killed the other never mates again. That's me. Basically I'm a solo item now."

Ann wasn't put off by the recitation; it reassured her. Margaret was letting her know she was an independent soul who valued independence in others. And that she was wounded, vulnerable, in spite of the cocky, self-assured exterior. Walking around and around the top deck the first night of the cruise, Ann found herself telling Margaret what she wanted in a partner for this later time in her life—not someone who would move in and smother her, but a woman who shared her interests, who wanted to travel some with a companion. "I've lived alone for a long time now," Ann said, "and I like solitude. I don't experience loneliness very often. I'm a pretty independent cuss. Had to be to get this far."

She smiles at her memories of that night. "We took one last turn around the deck and she turned to me and said, 'I *like* you,' just like that, with the emphasis on the like. I'm old enough to know what love is and I know it doesn't come the first day you meet somebody, so it was okay with me that she said 'like.' More than okay." She grins suddenly. "So I invited her back to my room."

How was it, I persist, how did you deal with your scar? Ann shrugs, shy now. "I said, Oh, the heck with it. I turned the light on and took my blouse off and said, 'Well, we might as well get this over with.' It was fine after that."

Sex and Our Past Lives

*I*f all of our scars were visible, dealing with them could be as straightforward as Ann and Margaret's experience. We could bare our chests, or run our fingers gently across a lover's scar. But what each of us has to deal with when we encounter another woman intimately for the first time is the scars and fears that are hidden, the expectations that are unnamed, and sometimes just the habits of a lifetime.

Buried experiences affect us just as surely as those habits and patterns we are aware of, but our lack of awareness of them means they can act like an undertow, pulling against the direction we are rowing in. These undertows can spring from a variety of sources.

For example, female gender patterning—wait to be asked, don't be sexually aggressive, don't *need* sex that much—a patterning that lesbians have inevitably inherited, may make us tentative when it comes to approaching another woman sexually or even when we want to initiate sex in an established relationship. You may have known since you were six that you liked girls better than boys, you may have called yourself a lesbian since puberty, but you still have been affected by the dominant culture, which tells us that boys ask girls for dates. Some of us deliberately incorporated the culture's male patterning when we were young, some of us worked at overcoming that patterning when we realized we weren't going to fit into the girl/boy model, some of us still wait to be asked—but each of us has had to deal with it in some way.

We also inherit family patterns in relation to our sexual expression. Wanda, who wants to go to medical school soon, was raised to believe her body was a wonderful gift and sexuality was a part of that gift. Nudity, masturbation, sexual expressions—they were normal, fun, and nice. The only inhibitions she ever experienced were around what it was and was not all right to do in public.

Kathryn, on the other hand, was raised in a family whose values were nearly the opposite. She was taught that masturbation was shameful, sex outside of matrimony was sinful, and nudity—well, it was never contemplated or discussed. In addition, when Kathryn first began to experience sexual feelings, she also was diagnosed with scoliosis, a curvature of the spine so severe and serious that she had to wear a body brace for nearly five years.

"I didn't date until I got to college," she remembers. "I never would have dated while I had the brace on. And when I began to figure out it was other girls I was attracted to, well, that wasn't written anywhere in the book our family followed." The first time Kathryn made love, she made sure she could undress in the dark with her back facing away from her partner. "I still have about a twenty-five percent curvature," she says. "It's pretty obvious when I'm naked or in a bathing suit. I was ashamed of my body's not being perfect. That's all."

When Kathryn began taking biology and anatomy/physiology courses in preparation for becoming a physical therapist, she realized she wanted to change some of her family patterning and her feelings about her spine. "Those values weren't my values anymore," she remembers, "and yet I was reacting to the nudity in some of my textbooks as if they were." At the same time, learning more about her body let Kathryn come to terms with her spine's "normal abnormality." "Lots of kids have it, is what I learned. What's to be ashamed of?"

When Kathryn and Wanda became lovers, those attitude adjustments served Kathryn well. "In fact, I doubt that we would have become lovers if I hadn't spent some time in therapy and in a lesbian discussion group talking about how I'd been raised to behave and how I wanted to behave myself, now that I was what we call 'grown-up.'"

Wanda admits privately that it is obvious to her that some of the sexual adventures that turn her on are harder for Kathryn—or they were at first. "I love to masturbate with a lover, with her watching me or touching my breasts while I bring myself to an orgasm. That's fun for me. Being watched is a turn-on. But it's something Kathryn has had to learn about." Wanda grins and admits, "She's willing, don't get me wrong. But I could tell it was new for her."

Issues that arise for a woman who has been a victim of sexual abuse in her childhood may not be conscious. Or—if she is aware of the past abuse—she may not be aware of how her present sexual behavior is related to her past. For the victims of such abuse—and for their partners—exploring sexuality can be like walking through a mine field, where the most innocent-appearing landscape can suddenly turn explosive. Women who have suffered rape or sexual abuse as adults generally know where the difficult areas are for them, and knowing this, they can communicate with lovers about what does and does not feel comfortable to them. Such communications may be difficult, but they are usually possible.

Barbara and Susan had never talked about sexual inhibitions. Susan assumed they were mutually uninhibited, in fact, since they both loved to dance until they were totally turned on and then would make love passionately. "It never occurred to me that someone as passionate as Barbara would have any areas of resistance," Susan said. "But one day we were playing around, I think we'd just gotten out of the shower. I was sitting on the bed and I grabbed her from behind and pulled her down on my lap. I was going to make love to her that way, from behind, kind of holding her arms down and playing with her. I was into anything new. We'd been living together for about three months and I was just starting to feel a little more sure of myself, you know?"

Barbara went absolutely rigid in Susan's arms. All of the playfulness was gone. "What's wrong?" Susan asked, and all Barbara could say was "You can't do that to me." *That*, they figured out, was holding Barbara's arms and touching her sexually.

Barbara told me it took months and months for her to understand what had happened. It bothered her enough to go into therapy. "I was overwhelmed by the feelings that surfaced for me that day. I had no idea where they were coming from, none. But I knew I didn't like the feelings. I didn't need to feel revolted by Susan's touching me, no matter how or where. I wanted to be free to love her and be loved by her, and something was stopping that."

Eventually, Barbara's memories of being sexually molested by her father and uncle when she was a small child began to surface, rise to consciousness. "They were both alcoholics and they had both been dead for quite a few years when I began to understand what had happened. It was my uncle who would hold me on his lap at night on the porch swing. He'd wrap his arms around me and push me down on his lap while he masturbated. I was terrified. I didn't know what was wrong with what we were doing, but I knew it *was* wrong. He'd breathe hard and I'd feel like I was going to be crushed." The physical patterning of Susan's arms around her from behind, sitting on a lap, and feeling sexual energy threw Barbara into a body memory of those early molestations. Her response to Susan was involuntary.

In the beginning, Susan and Barbara were both tempted to ignore what had happened. "I thought, well, we just won't do that again," admits Susan, "but that wasn't really a choice. It *had* happened, and we needed to know why. Barbara needed to know. I could tell that it was bothering her, even when we made love differently." Therapy, and later a support group she attended briefly, helped Barbara make her memories conscious so that her reactions—and her sexual expression—could be chosen.

Sexual Styles

"**B**utch/femme? It is alive and well today, let me tell you." Leslie leaned back in her chair and fixed me with an intense stare to see what I'd make of that. "Uh-huh," I said creatively. "Tell me what you mean."

"No matter how many of those Birkenstock-wearing, hairy-legged, women's studies lesbian feminists say we've evolved beyond butch and femme or we're working toward a more encompassing androgyny, the truth is, out here in the real world, butch and femme are the norm." Whew! Leslie and I may not agree exactly on the location of the real world, but her point of view is common with younger lesbians, I've found, and increasingly common with my own generation.

I am, I confess, one of those feminists who came out in the seventies and assumed that butch/femme was something lesbians did in the bad old days before Stonewall and feminism. There were no histories that explained the butch/femme phenomenon and it was not something that I understood viscerally. While it is still not something that figures in my life, I have read the histories that are available today and I listen carefully to my friends when they talk about the importance of butch/femme to their identities and relationships.

One common mistake, I hear them say, is that people think butch/femme is all about looks and fashion—if a woman's hair is long, she's a femme, if she wears a tie or bolero, she's butch.

"When I wear my black leather jacket and boots," says an eighteen-year-old lesbian with long blond hair, makeup, and dangling earrings, "I feel more powerful. And sexy. Then I'm being a butchy femme. I can flirt more easily. You know, let some girl know what I want." The other side of being a butchy femme is—you got it—being a femmy butch. That means, if I'm listening correctly, admitting the vulnerability of being more overtly aggressive in a relationship. "That's right," Leslie says. "The butch is taking the risk of initiating. Some of us admit that it's scary, some don't. For some of us, the risk of being rejected is part of the thrill, just as much as the thrill of having her say yes. For others, we're butch in spite of the risk. Me?" She sees the question I'm about to ask. "Me? I love it. I don't mind a rejection. Asking is what I like."

Margaret, who is sixty, has seen profound changes in the lesbian/gay scene during her lifetime. As a young butch in the fifties, she lived many of the expectations of her role. "In those days, being butch affected everything I did, how I dressed, how I made love, who I approached as a sexual partner."

Margaret felt the disdain of early feminists for the butch/femme way of life, but that isn't what changed it for her. "I'd already begun to relax some of the more ritualized aspects of being butch. I met Rachel in the early sixties. I think today they'd refer to her as an aggressive femme. The first time we made love, she informed me there was no way she was only going to be made love to. Not that she minded being the femme in bed, that was natural to her, but for her being femme meant being sexually aggressive. Not quite in the same way I was," Margaret smiled at the memory and wouldn't tell me more. "Over the years it just became more comfortable to have one person take charge of certain things. I know a lot of lesbians who do that, and for some it's about a role and for some not. Rachel was the cook, I washed the dishes. I did the laundry and she was responsible for upkeep on the cars. Things like that."

I asked Margaret if butch/femme figured in her new relationship with Ann. She laughs. "Have you asked Ann about that?" I haven't.

"She'll tell you it's ridiculous and that she doesn't want to have any-thing to do with such nonsense. But I'll tell you, yes, there is a lot of butch in me still, and if she's not a femme. . . . But it's something we don't talk about. Maybe we're old enough now just to live it, we don't have to name it."

"I think butch/femme has more to do with how we take care of one another, these days, than with dress codes or who initiates sex." Marty's thoughtful words let me know this was not a new subject for her. "I was a nun for twelve years. Basically that means I'm one of the world's all-time great caretakers. In my AA group they used to kid me about being the codependency poster child. I see that as a femme way of being. You know, 'Let me support you, dear, in being who you want to be, let me give you emotional and spiritual warmth in your strug-gles out there in the world.' Joan took care of me, too, but hers was more a physical caring. She'd do the chores, fix the cars, things that made her feel competent and good about herself at the same time she was helping me. When I was in balance and we were in balance together, it was a fine way to be; it was complementary."

Lesbians today are finding permission in themselves to experi-ment with a wide variety of sexual styles and practices. Sex clubs, s/m interactions, video porn, upscale dance and nightclubs—we have options our foremothers never dreamed of, or if they dreamed of them, they had fewer ways of actualizing their fantasies. Gay men have been changing their sexual practices in response to the AIDS epidemic, we are told; there are more long-term, monogamous gay male relationships. Lesbians, it seems, have grasped the pendulum too, but we are on the upswing, widening and redefining our sexual practices.

There is excitement in this opening out. And danger. One danger, of course, is that we will allow ourselves to be talked into something we're not ready for. It's easy to say, Be sure you know what you want, be sure and ask the right questions; but I have never found knowing what I want to be simple and I have surely not always known which questions were the right ones to help me get information with which I could evaluate a potentially fraught (if not dangerous) situation. Still, this is my responsibility. I accept it as such and do the best I can.

I asked every one of the eighteen women in my group of nine couples whether they had ever practiced sadomasochistic sex or if it was a part of their current sexual practice. Five said they had deliberately tried bondage play at least once—where one of the partners was tied or restrained while she was being made love to. Deborah and Margaret both said it was something from past relationships, not a current practice. For Wanda, bondage and other dominance/submission sex games had been part of her previous relationships and she hoped that they would be again someday with Kathryn, but they hadn't gotten to that level of intimacy yet. "I want us to feel totally comfortable with one another," said Wanda, "because that kind of power sharing is awesome and scary."

Leslie and Daphne were the only couple in this group of women who currently used s/m fantasy and practice as a part of their ongoing sexual relationship. "It is about intimacy," Daphne nods when I ask her about Wanda's perception. "Before I met Leslie, I thought I was the only one who had fantasies like that." Like what? I want to know. "Oh, you know. Where a strange woman who's drop-dead gorgeous walks into my bedroom and forces me into—well, into something I want to do but have trouble giving myself permission to do." Right. So how is it about intimacy? "You have to really trust your lover to tell her about those secret inner things, you know?"

Margaret agrees, to some extent, but in her fifty years of being a sexually active butch, she's seen the other side too. "I've known more women who used the role stuff to distance themselves from intimacy," she says. "If you put on the role like a mask and never take it off or let a lover see behind it, then I don't see it as anything but a protective device, something you use to distance yourself from the woman you're supposed to be making love with."

Like most discussions about sexual styles, there is no one way to be a lesbian. The atmosphere of comparison, judgment, and political correctness that sometimes surrounds this most private of choices seems misplaced to me.

Sex. When it is a shared, consensual activity, sex is fun. Scary.

Compelling. Intimate. It makes us feel powerful and shows us our vulnerability. Sex. We call it making love, and it can create love, this animalistic silliness, this breathing into one another's souls. Sex can transfigure everyday intimacy, transform lives. Sex. However we do it, when we do it with women, it's lesbian sex.

Safe Sex for Lesbians

"Safe sex?" Peggy asks. "I hear the younger ones talking about that, but Deb and I have been together ten years. We didn't think about those things. If I wasn't getting pregnant, that was safe enough for me." In the old days, we're told, sex was simple. If you both wanted to do it, you did it. I wish. And yet, there's some truth to that. The transmission of HIV was not an issue for lesbians in 1982 when Peggy and Deborah became lovers. Lesbians who had sex exclusively with women had a nonexistent level of the really bad STDs like syphilis and gonorrhea. Until herpes, we didn't really have much to worry about. And now there's AIDS.

"Of course I practice safe sex," Leslie nods. When I ask her what that means to her, she looks at me like I'm very slow to catch on. "Barriers. Latex barriers. I usually carry a dental dam, surgical gloves, maybe a condom, and sometimes finger cots. It all weighs about an ounce and fits in a small packet in my purse. I keep one in the glove compartment, too." I'm impressed. What about at home? I want to know. "Daphne and I aren't monogamous, but we've agreed to use barriers if we have other lovers. Then at home we don't have to worry. We both got tested last year," she's referring to a test for the presence of HIV antibodies in blood, "and we're both negative. So as long as we're safe outside the relationship, we'll be safe inside it." I nodded and thought: as long as you trust that your lover is being as careful outside the relationship as you are.

"No way would I have that kind of arrangement," protests Lisa when I tell her what Daphne and Leslie have decided. "First of all, I don't even trust myself that much. Why should Mariana trust me?" Now, instead of nodding, I'm shaking my head, no, I don't know what you mean. "Look, sex is one of the most unpredictable things humans do. It's about passion and lust. What's rational about that? How do I know I'd remember the dental dam when I finally slide down between her legs?" This I understand. It's one of the reasons heterosexuals end up with unwanted pregnancies. But isn't there a rather large difference between ending up pregnant and ending up dead, I want to know. "Not really," Mariana chimes in. "When you're not thinking, you're not thinking. And in my family," a first-generation immigrant family, "we were trying so hard to be middle-class Americans that pregnancy might have been worse than death. At least to hear my mother tell it."

Lisa and Mariana have been together for seven years. When they first became lovers in 1985, they'd heard of safe sex, but it wasn't clear to them what it consisted of. "We're African American and Latina," Mariana reminds me. "Sure, we knew from our communities that AIDS was around—mainly in the drug-using parts of the community. But other than not sleeping with men and not sharing needles, we had no idea what to do. And the AIDS test wasn't so available, was it?" It wasn't. "We *had* each had sex with a man during the year before we got together. So if there had been a test, I guess we might have done it."

Would you now? I asked them. If you weren't together for some reason, would you do safe sex with a new partner? "Oh, for sure," Mariana agrees easily. But Lisa isn't so sure. "I might." She shrugs. "But I really don't see how necessary it is for dykes. Down at the theater, there's a lot of talk about this and I may be stupid, but if you get HIV from semen or blood, it seems to me there's one easy way to be safe with another woman and that's: don't go down on her when she's bleeding. You know what I mean? Everything else seems a little far-fetched."

I do know what Lisa means. Like, if she's not menstruating, I might get infected with the AIDS virus *if* I go down on a woman who's just had unprotected sex with an HIV-positive man *if* I'm doing it within a few hours of her last sexual encounter and *if* I swallow some of the semen or have a cut in my mouth. In my life, this is not likely to happen, but it could. I'd be more likely to be struck by lightning, but it *could* happen.

"Wrong," says Leslie, my nonmonogamous dating expert. "Vaginal fluids are just like semen. Why do lesbians resist dealing with reality?"

Leslie is wrong. Vaginal fluids act more like saliva than semen. Vaginal fluids and saliva inhibit potentially infectious things.[5] Vaginal fluids act to protect a delicate area of our anatomy, just as saliva does. Very young women—preteens and early teenagers—are at greater risk for HIV infection because the walls of their vaginas, which are lined by the mucous membranes that produce vaginal fluid, are thinner and contain fewer immunity-producing cells than those of women in their mature childbearing years.[6] In postmenopausal women, the vagina walls again begin to thin and vaginal dryness is more common.

Lesbians aren't resisting dealing with reality, we just haven't had access to a lot of accurate information. "So what's a girl to do?" asks Marty, the ex-nun, who has just ended a fifteen-year monogamous relationship. "I'm forty-six years old. I may never have another relationship, but I hope I do. And if I do, I don't have a clue what's going to be required of me. Is she going to start asking me if I use dental dams? I mean, I've never even *seen* one, let alone experimented with one."

Dental dams are not high on the official safe-sex-practices list this year. Neither the Centers for Disease Control (CDC) nor the New York State Department of Health has taken a position on dental dams (or cut-up condoms or plastic household wrap) for use in oral sex on a woman. Why? Because they haven't been tested and because they aren't "containers" in the way that a condom is. (After ejaculating, a man can slip the condom off and tie it, containing the dangerous semen. You know where the semen is and which side of the condom is in and which out.) Dental dams are only a barrier until they slip off at a crucial moment or are dropped on the floor in the heat of whatever. ("Oh, God," she moaned, "which side was me and which was her?") They give an illusion of safety that may be more dangerous than simply paying attention to things like the presence of blood or open sores. If dental dams turn you on, though, some sex stores do sell panties with open crotches and devices to fasten the dental dam into place.

If you have open cuts or sores on your hands, and if you are unsure of your HIV status or that of your partner, then Latex gloves or finger cots are a good idea. They may protect you from HIV and other STDs like herpes, and they may protect the woman you are making love to from your blood.

Some women have told me, "I just won't sleep with anyone new until we've both been tested. Until then, we can have plenty of hot sex with our clothes on. This is not something I need to die for." This stance takes care of the HIV risk, but not herpes or other STDs. Other women have said they know what safe sex is, but no one in their circle is practicing it. "No. No one. My roommate and I have a whole bag of dental dams. Thirty-six of them. We use them as cat toys."

"The thing that makes the most sense to me is defining safe sex as conversation." Joan, who was Marty's partner for fifteen years and is only recently single, has thought about the future. "Most of the women I meet these days I meet at my AA meeting. I'm astonished at how protected my life has been. I mean, I'm an alcoholic, sure, but for me drinking was something I did with Marty. The stories I hear at the women's and the gay/lesbian meetings have shown me how sheltered I've been. And I intend to stay that way. But I can imagine falling in love with someone who hasn't lived as safe a life as me. What I'm saying is, given the backgrounds of the women I'm meeting, I've thought a lot about safe sex."

I ask Joan what she means by safe sex as conversation. "Well, talking about our histories is part of it. But I don't mean just that. I know anybody can lie. I did, while I was drinking." I agree that I wouldn't begin to know how to assess information about a potential lover's past. In fact, it seems vaguely useless to me, if not dangerous. I tell Joan a story Leslie told me about a woman she'd seen briefly just after she and Daphne began to live together. They'd talked about safe sex and the woman assured Leslie she had never slept with a man or done IV drugs. Leslie insisted on using a glove and a condom on her dildo anyway, because of the promise she'd made to Daphne, even though she admits it seemed safe enough at the time, and if she'd had only herself to think about, she might have said forget it. "I found out later the woman was a health-care worker, an intern actually, and she had a lot of patients who were HIV positive. I couldn't have found any dyke with a higher risk factor, and yet it never occurred to me to ask that question."

Joan is nodding thoughtfully. "I hear what you're saying. I guess what I mean by conversation and safe sex is more about me, setting up an atmosphere in which I don't feel awkward about taking care of myself, however I decide to do that."

Finally, each lesbian must make her own decision about the level of risk she is comfortable with. We all take risks every day. Getting in our car to drive to work is a risk. Some mornings we're tired enough or distracted enough to recognize this; other mornings we never think about it. We're more likely to die while driving to work than because we've had unprotected sex with another woman. The assertion that we can prevent either of these untimely demises is probably true; but it is also true that most of us don't want to live our lives from such a protected stance. We prefer to take the small risks and accept the consequences. The alternatives are too limiting—would we ever go out of our homes if we were afraid of what might happen to us outside of it? We'd never drive a car or fly in an airplane; and most of us *want* to do the things that taking those risks allows.

Lesbians need correct information about how HIV is transmitted, exactly what acts could transmit it and with what likelihood. Without that information, we may be like a woman living in a relatively safe neighborhood who treats the environment outside her home like bombed-out Sarejevo. As women, we have a long history of being told we shouldn't enjoy sex, that sex is for men and procreation is for women. As lesbians, we have a long history of being told that the sexual expression of our love is shameful and disgusting. We don't need to tell ourselves and one another that it is never safe to be sexually spontaneous.

To say that most lesbians who are HIV positive probably got the virus from shared needles or from sex with an HIV-infected man is *not* to say they are not lesbians and do not need or deserve support from the lesbian community. Those lesbians won't be put in a CDC category that says "Lesbian" because no such category exists. They will be dumped, statistically, into the categories of women who are IV drug users or of women who are infected through heterosexual transmission. Lesbians with AIDS are lesbians, and whatever happens to us "statistically" when we test HIV positive, we need to make sure that being dumped out of the lesbian community, however we define that, is not one of the side effects.

And to say that lesbian sex is really pretty safe compared to other risks we take in our daily lives is also not to abandon the gay men who are struggling with a much more serious sexual risk factor. The AIDS crisis has affected every homosexual person, and that has occurred because of homophobia, because the world out there does not distinguish between gay men and lesbians.

But we know the difference. And we need to protect our lesbian community from sex-negative messages that are unwarranted and from paranoia about sex at the same time we are recognizing that the struggle against homophobia generated by the AIDS crisis is one we share with gay men.

REFERENCES

1. Lennard J. Davis, "Text Sex," *The Nation*, March 29, 1993, pp. 418–20.

2. Lillian Faderman, *Odd Girls and Twilight Lovers: A History of Lesbian Life in Twentieth-Century America*. New York: Viking Penguin, 1991.

3. Judith McDaniel, *Just Say Yes*. Ithaca, N.Y.: Firebrand Books, 1991.

4. Toni Morrison, *The Bluest Eye*. New York: Pocket Books, 1972, pp. 102–104.

5. P. Greenhouse, "Female-to-Female Transmission of HIV," *Lancet*, August 15, 1987, 401–402, and L. R. Peterson, L. Doll, C. White, and S. Chu, "No Evi-

dence for Female-to-Female HIV Transmission Among 960,000 Female Blood Donors," *Journal of AIDS*, 1992, Vol. 5, No. 9, 853–55, and "Lesbians Safe from AIDS Transmission," *Lancet*, July 23, 1994, in press.

Scientists from Turin University, Italy, said they had found in a six-month study that various forms of oral and anal lesbian sex did not pass on the HIV virus. They studied 18 lesbian couples in steady relationships in which one partner carried the AIDS virus and the other had tested negative for HIV. Although most took part in what scientists consider risky sex, there was no evidence of woman-to-woman transmission during the study. The risky practices were defined as orogenital sex, anal manipulation, sex during a woman's monthly period, the sharing of sex toys, and the use of a technique known as rimming, or oral stimulation of the anus.

6. "UN Finds Teen-Age Girls at High Risk of AIDS," *The New York Times*, July 30, 1993.

RESOURCES

Books on Sexual Practices

Judith Barrington, editor, *An Intimate Wilderness: Lesbian Writers on Sexuality*. Portland, Oregon: Eighth Mountain Press, 1991. Essays, stories, and poems give an overview of a complex subject.

Susie Bright, *Susie Sexpert's Lesbian Sex World*. Pittsburgh, Pa.: Cleis Press, 1990. Hilarious essays on lesbian sex from the self-named lesbian sex guru.

———, *Susie Bright's Sexual Reality*, Pittsburgh, Pa.: Cleis Press, 1992. More essays on a wide range of subjects, from dildos to men to lesbians with HIV.

Leslie Feinberg, *Stone Butch Blues*. Ithaca, N.Y.: Firebrand Books, 1993. This novel explores one woman's experience of growing up as a transgendered person and coming out as a butch in the bars of the prefeminist sixties.

Elizabeth Kennedy and Madeline Davis, *Boots of Leather, Slippers of Gold: The History of a Lesbian Community*. New York: Routledge, 1993. A nonfiction exploration of the lesbian bar culture from the 1930s to the early 1960s, with special emphasis on class and the butch/femme scene.

Joanne Loulan, *Lesbian Sex*. Minneapolis, MN: Spinsters Ink, 1984. A comprehensive overview of what we do and under what conditions. Chapters on practical exercises as well as more theoretical discussion of coming out, disability, aging, motherhood, and more.

Lesbian Passion: Loving Ourselves and Each Other. Minneapolis, MN: Spinsters Ink,

1987. Less practical matters and more discussion of self-esteem, couples, recovery, and celibacy make this a more issue-oriented book.

The Lesbian Erotic Dance: Butch, Femme, Androgyny, and Other Rhythms. Minneapolis, MN: Spinsters Ink, 1990. A summary of many questionnaires in which lesbians answered questions about butch and femme, among other issues. Much of the theoretical framework of the book originated at a Toronto conference panel featuring Deb Edel, Madeline Davis, Jewelle Gomez, Sue Golding, Amber Holibaugh, Liz Kennedy, Joan Nestle, and Esther Newton.

Catalogs

For catalogs of sex toys and other pleasures, consult the advertising pages of any of the new lesbian magazines and newspapers that now exist from coast to coast.

To get you started—two of the oldest pleasure catalogs. They come discreetly wrapped. Both offer sexual aids, oils, safe-sex-for-lesbians information and devices, videos, and more. Good Vibrations also has a Sexuality Library catalog.

Eve's Garden
119 West 57th Street, Suite 420
New York, NY 10019
Send $3.00

Good Vibrations
938 Howard Street, Suite 101
San Francisco, CA 94103

PART THREE

Living as Lesbians

The Homophobia Thing

*L*esbians are as different from one another as any fantasist could possibly imagine—except in one crucial factor: we all choose women as our life partners, our intimate partners, our sexual partners. That choice, its joys, puzzles, and difficulties, brings us into an entirely different life arena than choosing a partner of the opposite sex does. That choice makes us outsiders, generally unsupported by the social fabric of the predominant heterosexual culture. While many of us like the view from without, indeed find our energy and joy for life in our difference, we should also recognize that we must continually push against the social norms. There are few approved role models or mentors for lesbians, whether as single lesbians or as couples.

It is perhaps appropriate that our knowledge of the sexual nature of some of our foremothers' relationships comes from an inquisitorial document detailing a criminal offense. Judith Brown's account of the trial of Abbess Benedetta[1] reminds us that there are centuries-old reasons for hiding our sexual orientation. This fear is realistic. And it harms us by giving rise to heterosexism.

Heterosexism—the assumption that everyone is heterosexual—is what lesbians face when we are ignored, when we can find little or no reflection of ourselves in popular culture, no mention of us when hot national political issues like health care are discussed, when we are seldom included in the daily life of our culture, our "civilization." It isn't only that my lover can't be covered by my health insurance policy from my place of employment, but Hallmark doesn't publish a card that celebrates our anniversary or the anniversaries of our friends. Sometimes we recognize the large omissions and forget the small ones that we deal with every day, but they are there, the opposite of support—those small details that whittle away at our sanity and our staying power like grains of sand carving caverns out of hard rock.

Heterosexism is, on the one hand, fairly benign; it is an omission, not a direct attack. And it is changing—fairly rapidly in some aspects. When I came out, I could not have expected to see a television news special on the phenomenon of gay parenting, nor would I have expected a program about the thriving lesbian community in Northampton. There were only two lesbian feminist presses operating in the United States when I came out; today there are more than a dozen feminist or women's presses that specialize in lesbian literature and culture. We can choose a gay/lesbian tour or travel agent, stay in gay/lesbian or "friendly" guest houses, motels, dude ranches, or resorts. The list expands every day.

It is important that heterosexism is fading away, even when our visibility as lesbians makes us feel vulnerable and exposed, because the inevitable companion of heterosexism is homophobia—the fear of same-sex intimacy. Homophobia is what lesbians face when we are portrayed as vicious, oversexed demons in films or, in the words of Pat Robertson at the Republican National Convention in 1992, as women who would murder our children.[2] Homophobia insists that all things lesbian or gay be kept quiet, hidden, secret. That secrecy allows homophobic images to define the norm of lesbian and gay existence and gives permission for the violence against lesbians and gay men perpetrated by homophobic people.

Sometimes it is difficult to see where we should or can break the homophobia cycle. We are afraid of being attacked, so we hide our lives. When we hide, society assumes we don't exist. When we don't exist, we aren't known. And so the fear and hatred of the unknown becomes fear and hatred of us, and the old myths and distortions about who we are define us in the popular mind.

A modern example of this vicious circle, one that reminds us homophobia isn't gone yet, has been the national "debate" about whether or not gay people should be included in the military. Until recently, court-martial and removal from military service was what awaited anyone suspected of being lesbian or gay. Now there is allegedly a policy referred to as "Don't ask, don't tell." But if you do tell, you can still be court-martialed, which only maintains or exacerbates the expectation of secrecy about lesbian and gay lives.

The discussion about whether or not we could serve in the military was, of course, ridiculous, since we have always been a part of the military. Gay men who hid their sexual orientation served. Lesbians as well as heterosexual women passed as men in order to serve in the Revolutionary War and the Civil War and probably in every other conflict in which this country has ever been involved. So the terms of the debate were not accurately being stated.

The *real* question is whether lesbians and gays serving in the military will ever be allowed to say who they are openly or whether they will continue to be required to hide. The real debate is about heterosexism, which would ignore our presence, and homophobia, which would allow us to be harassed and attacked if we were noticed or if we said who we were.

If every lesbian and gay man in the military felt safe enough to say, "I'm lesbian or I'm gay," American society might have to examine some cherished myths about us. If lesbians have been living with and working with heterosexual women without "hitting" on them, if taking a shower with a lesbian has not placed the daughters of America in sexual jeopardy, at the very least those heterosexual women who discover they have lesbian friends or coworkers will not shudder with horror when the lesbian myths are waved at them.

Suzanne Pharr[3] and Cynthia Enloe[4] have each written about how fear of homosexuals (lesbians) has been used to keep heterosexual women in their gender-limited identities. Most recently, Enloe observed that the group that would gain the most if homosexuals were allowed to serve openly in the military was not lesbians, not gay men, but heterosexual women. The fear of being thought of as lesbian keeps heterosexual women from reporting male sexual harassment and violence. The woman who complains about a man's sexual interest is immediately labeled "lesbian" and subjected to investigation and possible court-martial. Married heterosexual women have been court-martialed with dishonorable discharges because they did not abide closely enough to the feminine stereotype.

I understand the dynamics of homophobia, but I'm always surprised when heterosexuals of good will, those folks who say they are our allies, don't understand why secrecy is painful to us. They ask, "Why do you have to tell people you're a lesbian? Why do you want them to know about your sex life like that?" As though we were exhibitionists, we lesbians who are out. My response is simple. "Do you tell people you're married and introduce them to your wife?" I asked one male friend that question. He nodded, not seeing my point. "Then you're giving far more information than when I say I'm homosexual. You're telling me your sexual orientation *and* that you're currently having sex *and* with which woman."

His sense that I was revealing more than my sexual orientation involved "the secret," of course. Bringing a secret into the light of day always carries more power than acknowledging a known fact.

When lesbians are in a relationship, and when we are public about the nature of that relationship, we have to face the effect of our sexuality in the world. A single lesbian can be seen as a single woman—the world may assume that she's not having sex—and so she's not quite so threatening. This was my experience as a single lesbian dealing with some heterosexuals and most institutions, such as the college where I taught occasionally. Most people in my life know I'm a lesbian, but when I'm not "coupled" and they don't have to inquire about my partner or spend time with us together, then I'm "just Judith." When we are coupled, our sexuality is out there, known or assumed, but it can't be ignored.

The Closet

Closeting is the act or process by which a lesbian or gay person hides sexual orientation. Closets come in all designs. Some have revolving doors for those who are out of the closet in one setting—going openly with friends to a gay bar or concert, for example—but in the closet in other settings—as at work or in a church community or as a Girl Scout leader. Other closets have transparent doors, allowing those with the secret password to see that the person is lesbian. When Susan, who was married to a man at the time, found herself attracted to Barbara at a NOW meeting, she let Barbara know how much she liked women's music. She did like it and she'd heard some lesbian musicians on the local college radio station's women's program, too. Susan casually mentioned Meg Christian and Chris Williamson. Barbara was surprised that this "straight" woman was talking about lesbian culture, but she got the real message pretty quickly.

Codes vary from group to group, class to class, and in different parts of the country. Cracking the code in San Francisco might not serve you very well in Des Moines.

The convention of the closet requires that if you meet a woman you know as a lesbian (because she made a pass at you at the gay bar last night), and if she is with someone you don't know, you can't refer to her lesbianism openly. Unless she does. But when she is under the same restraint, not knowing whether you are willing for a stranger, her companion, to know you are a lesbian, conversation can be very difficult.

When I came out as a lesbian, that is, began my first affair with a woman, I decided that I didn't want to hide, and generally this choice has served me well. It has not always been easy, and sometimes I have chosen to be closeted, but being open about who I am lets me be easier in myself than when I have hidden.

That "coming out" summer marked a year of transition for me. I felt as if I had created myself a new person, and that feeling was helped by moving to a new community to a new job, teaching at a small liberal arts college in a rural community. When one of the women in the department of the college where I was teaching asked me, early in my first semester, if I was married or living with someone, I told her that I was a lesbian and currently single. She looked at me with some shock and asked how I thought I would fit into this community. Her tone of voice implied that I couldn't. In fact, I never did, and I was denied tenure six years later, a result I attribute directly to being an out lesbian in a conservative academic environment. My father had an assessment of the situation that was painful for me at the time, but seems accurate to me today. "You made some choices along the way," he said, "and basically you chose not to get tenure there." He's right. If I'd wanted tenure I would have played the game and been closeted.

Being closeted has its own problems, of course. It can make it difficult for lesbians to find one another (in spite of our finely tuned radar). Some of us are used to hiding, and part of this is generational. Women who have been closeted, who grew up as lesbians believing their only safety was in being closeted, have practiced not looking like "stereotypical lesbians," not wearing the dyke haircut or the telltale labyris. Safety lay in passing, in being mistaken for straight. Fifteen years ago, when I lived on a farm and went into the local village, I was astonished at how many of the women seemed like dykes to me. They weren't. They were farm women, wives mostly, who wore their barn boots and flannel shirts straight from the barn to the bank or grocery store. Because they were married, they could afford to look like dykes. The few lesbians in the village, whom I did eventually meet, were carefully feminine. They taught elementary school or worked in the library. They didn't dare give another woman "the look."

As a result, many of the lesbian relationships in that time and place were circumscribed. Once safely over the tension of "is she or isn't she?" these women seldom changed partners. Or if they did change partners, it was a swap from within the closely knit, tightly concealed circle of lesbians they'd known for years. In a group of ten lesbians, you could count on eight of them being ex-lovers with someone else (or two or three someone elses) in the group.

This still happens, in spite of the freedom to cruise and choose. "My ex-lover's lover is my roommate's ex-lover," a young friend told me recently. Once inside a circle of safety, once having identified which women are lesbians, we seem reluctant to leave it—our women's studies class, our twelve-step group, the softball team, they all seem to have the same intense ratio of ex-lovers and soon-to-be-lovers. The pattern is, in the larger sense of the word, incestuous; it breeds homogeneity, it denies difference, the need for differences, which keep us sharp and interested. And interesting. It is an old pattern, raised out of old issues. It is a current pattern, persisting because of homophobia.

Sometimes the pattern makes it hard for us to find one another. Deborah and Peggy, the couple from Washington, D.C., met at work. "It's not like I was going to run into her down at the gym where she was lifting weights," Deborah reminds me, stressing that *she* was not the athletic type. "We were both in our twenties and had done our time with men. I got two kids out of it and she had a two-year-old. When you hear a sister complaining about a man, it doesn't usually mean much, but with Peg, well, I felt like she was trying to tell me something." They danced around *it* for nearly a year and then decided to take a vacation together. "No kids, nobody from work looking at you sideways when you're trying to talk, it didn't take us more than an hour to figure it out after we got off alone together." It was Peggy's first relationship with a woman, but Deborah had been having affairs with women since junior high school. "I really liked Peggy," Deborah admits, "and I didn't want to do anything that would scare her away. If I told her I was gay, how was I to know she'd still be speaking to me the next day?"

This is the issue that heterosexuals seeking romance don't ever face. True, a man can tell a woman he's interested in her sexually or romantically, and she might never speak to him again, but it won't be because of his sexuality. She may not like his style, his looks, the way he spoke to her, or a hundred other maybes, but she won't fault him for being a heterosexual.

But for a woman who wants to find a woman—unless they are both open about their lesbianism—there is always the question, "If I tell her I'm a lesbian, what will happen to this budding friendship?" With luck, she'll be thrilled. Marty was. This ex-nun was in the audience at a feminist conference when Joan did a workshop presentation on women starting their own businesses. "I'd seen her the day before at the opening session of the conference," Marty confessed, "and I couldn't think how to approach her. She looked too high-powered just to walk up to and start chatting. She was busy and seemed important; lots of women knew her." Marty couldn't tell from Joan's workshop whether Joan was gay or straight, she just knew she was attracted to her. After the workshop Marty thought of a question about her own situation, living rurally, that involved more time than Joan had right after the workshop. They made a date for coffee later in the day.

"I thought she was really cute," Joan admits. "I'd been involved with one woman very briefly and—let's face it—I was really, really horny. Then this woman, who I thought was coming on to me, tells me she's just left the convent. I mean, it was 1975. Who ever heard of lesbian nuns then?" Joan considered being careful and keeping the conversation businesslike. "But finally I said to myself, what the hell. I wasn't having coffee with her because I wanted to talk about business. I was attracted to her. In the middle of describing how she might start a little bed-and-breakfast business out of her home, I just blurted out that I was a lesbian. Something about how glad I'd be to stay in a place like that."

"Right," Marty remembers, laughing. "All of a sudden the conversation went from nowhere to very, very interesting. I let her know I'd be interested in an on-site consultation, and she came up the next weekend." And moved upstate just a few months later.

Among younger lesbians, particularly those in the middle and upper classes, being out is easier today than it was when Joan and Marty met in the mid-seventies. Mariana and Lisa, who became lovers in college in 1987, never felt any particular need to hide their relationship in that environment, and they report that it is even more acceptable today on many college campuses. Some older lesbians look cynically on these young women, wondering if their lesbianism will survive their women's studies degrees and graduation into the real world.

"Oh, for the most part, I think it will," says Leslie seriously. She graduated from Radcliffe in 1985. "We're in an easier place about gender issues, for one thing. Younger women feel okay about playing with butch and femme, and frankly you don't have to be gay to want to mess up gender stereotypes. Punk, butch/femme, transgender stuff . . . " she shrugs. "Younger people don't have such an *attitude* about it all. It makes it easier to just be who you are. Open, you know, not closeted about anything."

In a recent book, Michelangelo Signorile says the convention of the closet reinforces antigay loathing and gay self-loathing. For gay people, being in the closet hurts "themselves and all other queers. The invisibility they perpetuate harms us more than any of their good deeds might benefit us." And if I, as a gay person, cooperate in keeping another gay's secret, he insists, I am being "codependent with those whose dysfunction enables the bigots who bash us."[5] This is the basis on which Signorile advocates "outing" lesbians and gays who are public figures, but are closeted. Outing is the term that has come to refer to publicly disclosing a person's homosexuality without their permission or cooperation.

I think this view of closeting is too simple. The closet *is* a response to the intersection of two things that affect gay people. One of them is, as Signorile suggests, the loathing that society in general seems to have for us, which some of us have—sadly, inevitably—incorporated into our own self-image. The other strand of that intersection, however, is fear.

What a society loathes it attempts to destroy. And even if I have escaped the snares of self-loathing, I know very well that I am not safe walking the streets of America as an out lesbian. I think women can perhaps understand this more easily than men. As a woman, I am not safe walking many of the streets of America, either, and that has nothing to do with whether or not I love my sex, my self. There are trails I will not hike by myself, streets I will not walk down. I make these realistic assessments every day, and they are not based on self-loathing. It may be true that, if every woman walked exactly where she wanted every day, there would be so many of us out there walking that no one would dare attack or harass us. But frankly I doubt it.

The fear that keeps lesbians and gays closeted is of two kinds. The most obvious is a fear for our lives, our physical well-being. We are bombarded regularly with stories of lesbian and gay people, basically minding their own business, who are thrown off bridges, shot to death in national forests, beaten to death in public restrooms, and stabbed while lounging at the beach. We read of homes fire-bombed, children threatened, businesses destroyed. The other fear is less specific. We "fear" not being able to do the things we want to do in life because that one part of who we are—our sexuality—will define us and limit us by society's understanding of that definition. Most human beings want to be more than their sexuality. We do want our sexuality, free, unfettered by shame or legal restrictions, but we want far more than that for our lives.

When I moved to a rural area, I decided to work with the Girl Scouts again. I'd been a scout when I was growing up and loved the opportunities scouting opened up for me. I wanted to take a group of girls winter camping in the snow, canoeing in the summer. Although I've never had children of my own, finding ways for children to be part of my life has been important to me. So I became an assistant troop leader in the village I lived in, and in summers I led wilderness canoe trips up in the Adirondack lakes. It was fun. Not the most important thing I was doing, but fun. I couldn't have done it if I had been public—in that village—about being a lesbian. I lived with a woman. I was openly a lesbian in the larger town where I taught. My partner and I started a lesbian-feminist publishing company out of our garage, then a lesbian poetry-reading series that was advertised discreetly by mail. But to the Girl Scouts, I was closeted.

I was closeted, not out of self-loathing or dysfunction, but because of an accurate assessment of what was possible in that time and place. True, the effect of my choosing not to say the word *lesbian* out loud did nothing to counter the loathing those villagers probably harbored toward lesbian and gay people. When those girls grow up, they will not have known an adult who said openly and comfortably that she was a lesbian. Signorile says that closeting is not morally neutral but reinforces the view that being gay is a disgusting secret. But if I had said that I was a lesbian, they would not have known me at all, and their parents would have made sure that they knew the reasons— that "women like that" are disgusting, perverted. As a result, I don't see this issue in simple black-and-white terms. We did have some great canoe trips, those girls and I.

Meanwhile, in the larger town where I was teaching, everyone knew I was a lesbian. I was open in my department, I taught a lesbian literature course, I insisted that my partner be invited to any faculty event where "spouses" were included. When I was fired, what was the message given to my lesbian and gay students? They told me what the message was; "You're really being punished for this, aren't you?" Some of them saw the negative example of what happened to me and chose not to be out; they wrapped their fear more tightly about them, and with it, possibly, an extra layer of self-loathing and dysfunction.

After listening to Signorile's arguments about why lesbians and gays shouldn't remain closeted and why it is a moral act to out someone in public life who is closeted, a friend said that this behavior reminded her of some of the Christian fundamentalists she'd grown up among. "They're moralists," she stressed, "gays outing others or fundamentalists pointing at sin—they both presume they can judge your behavior for you, better than you can. When I was a girl, if someone in the church community didn't like your behavior, they'd go to your home and tell you how to be better and they'd shame you in the larger community. I know Signorile says he's reacting against a 'shameful secret,' but I don't see much difference between being shamed by the church in front of the community and being outed by someone like Signorile because he thinks you're being shameful. As far as I'm concerned, they both use shameful methods."

It seems to me there are enough shameful things in the world that we don't need to exacerbate the problem. I wish every lesbian and gay person could live openly. It is what I prefer for myself, and at the same time, I know it has not always been completely possible for me. Being out is a goal and a process. For this process to work, like almost every other process in life, we have to undertake it for ourselves. No one can do it for us, nor can we do it for others. Outing makes no sense to me when it refers to something we do to others. Being out, as a choice, can actually make sense of our lives.

Opening Our Own
Closet Doors

Recent surveys and polls tell us that coming out of the closet does lead to greater acceptance of lesbian and gay people. *U.S. News* reports that 73 percent of those who know a gay person favor equal rights for lesbians and gays, whereas only 55 percent of those who don't know (or don't know they know) a gay person favor equal rights.[6] In less than ten years, the number of people surveyed who personally know a gay or lesbian has grown from 25 percent of Americans to 53 percent. That increase is a marker for the thousands upon thousands of lesbians and gays who have chosen the risk of openness over the suffocation of the closet. That statistic alone would be enough for us to understand why gays and lesbians, as a movement, need to challenge ourselves to be open about who we are whenever and wherever we can.

I've lived long enough, been out publicly as a lesbian long enough, to be able to cite many examples of how people's attitudes toward lesbians became more positive when they found out that they actually knew one. A woman I once cotaught a course with was hostile and challenging toward me in front of our students, in spite of the fact that she had invited *me* to work with *her*. Later, she confessed I was the first lesbian she had ever known, and when we began working together, she was afraid I would hit on her. She came from a fairly conservative Christian background, one she'd rejected years before, but in spite of this rejection and her subsequent intellectual training, her initial response to me was an emotional throwback to her earlier lessons. Today, she is a friend who knows that lesbians aren't prowling around looking for unsuspecting straight women, but she had to know one to make that leap.

Time published an article on "Coming Out in the Country,"[7] which featured the youth minister of the First Congregational Church in Corvallis, Oregon. The Reverend Lois Van Leer and her partner, Karen, have survived despite death threats and accusations of being witches who perform animal sacrifices. In the face of that, Van Leer still insists, "You just have to decide that if you don't speak out now, it'll only get worse." And she is right for herself and the life she has chosen. I do think it is important to notice that she and her lover had lived in this town for a long time before they came out. They had a base of support, they were surrounded by people who knew them and their work, as a result of many years of living shoulder to shoulder. If Lois and Karen had moved to Corvallis as out lesbians, I doubt the opportunity to be known in that way would have been available to them. And there was a bonus for the people who have supported these two lesbians from within the community. This coming out gave the people of Corvallis an opportunity to be "better" than they might have expected themselves to be if they were questioned abstractly about the "issue" of homosexuality.

Knowing these things, assessing the possibilities, and making the best choices for our lives requires courage and maturity. Lesbians, unlike heterosexuals, have these choices to make every day: we have to weigh how open to be in which situation. Living and working in almost complete openness, as my partner and I do today, is a hard-earned gift. We don't hide the fact that we are lesbians or that we are in a relationship. We introduce one another as "partner" in professional as well as social settings. We *are* discreet. I think there is a difference between being closeted and erecting a privacy screen around our relationship. I don't hold her hand when we take our evening walk, but we walk close together, our arms brushing. But then, I haven't seen anyone in this neighborhood except some teenagers walking around holding hands.

When Jan and I decided to have a ceremony of commitment, I realized that this ceremony would not have been possible ten years ago, certainly not possible in 1975, when I began my first lesbian "marriage." I did not have the broad support in my community that I have today. Even though I was out at the college where I was teaching, I knew there was a great deal of hostility toward me there. Inviting fellow faculty members to a lesbian wedding was not on my list of possible things to do in those days.

Does it matter to me that it is possible today? Absolutely. "Our hearts have been changed," I wrote in a poem we used in the program for our ceremony, "by what has transpired." In some indefinable way, as heterosexual couples who decide to marry have always known, making promises to one another in front of our community has changed our basic outlook about our relationship. We are married. We mean to test the limits of ourselves and our relationship within our understanding of the meaning of that concept—marriage. We have said to ourselves, to one another, and to our community that this is not a casual relationship, that this is in fact a life commitment, that we are choosing one another and we want our community to support us in this choice. We also wanted to reclaim the word *marriage*—there is no other that describes a physical, emotional, and spiritual union between two people. And finally, we wanted to erase some of the secrecy about lesbian relationships that can be so damaging to us. In the words we wrote for the celebration, we asked our family, friends, and community "to affirm the reality of this marriage, to refuse with us the secrecy so often associated with our relationships that renders us invisible and works to make our relationships less important, less permanent."

Response from the various sectors of our community was mixed, ranging from wild enthusiasm to quiet support, to disapproving silence, to outright disapproval. Because I was a member of a Quaker meeting, we considered having a formal marriage "under the care of the meeting," which would have meant my entire Quaker community supported my marriage. This was not possible because of the range of response, but the support we received was far greater than the negation. As a result, we had a Quaker wedding in the meeting house with many members of the meeting in attendance, but the marriage was not officially "under the care of the meeting."

Lesbians also questioned our decision to have a ceremony, to use the word *marriage*, to use the word *faithful*, and to exchange rings—words and gestures perceived as patriarchal, as oppressive to women. Some wondered why we had chosen to be so public; why not a private ceremony in our home? We talked about all of these choices, gladly, openly, and at length.

Finally, it was not only Jan's and my hearts that were changed by what we experienced that day, but friends and family members who were there have told us they, too, were changed by taking part in this ceremony. "I was surprised," admitted a longtime friend who is a lesbian. "I didn't expect to be moved by it." What moved her, she decided after a while, was realizing how important that wide support for a relationship might be. Heterosexual friends have thanked us for letting them be a part of our experience. "It was like any other marriage," one said. "Somehow I thought it would be different." And Jan's adult children publicly welcomed me into their family, which has affected the dynamics of my relationships with them and our expectations of one another.

It does matter that we could have a public celebration of our relationship: it means that there are more possibilities today for lesbians and gays to open the closet door. Woman by woman, man by man, we have had the courage to be open about who we are.

This openness, inevitably, has caused a backlash. The idea of lesbian and gay marriage seemed to be the glue of hatred that held together the Republican National Convention. It is the fuel that has energized the antigay constitutional amendment in Colorado, and will put a similar initiative on the ballot in many states in 1994. "Give them equal housing protection," said religious conservatives in Albany, New York, last year, "and next they'll be pushing for the right to get married, have children, and be called family."

Yes. That's right. We will.

As a lesbian who wants to find another lesbian, you will have to learn to negotiate the closet and deal with homophobia. Even if you decide from the first moment of realizing you're a lesbian that you love that identity and intend to be completely open about who you are in the world, not everyone else will have come to exactly the same conclusion, at least not at exactly the same moment. But if you are willing to say you're a lesbian, at least other women who might be interested in you won't be in doubt about your orientation. That's a giant step forward.

One major obstacle couples need to negotiate is how out they each want to be, in their communities, their families, their relationships. If Margaret and Ann had met earlier in their lives, and Ann had been committed to being closeted to protect her daughter and Margaret had needed to be out to protect her sense of who she was, theirs would have been a very difficult relationship. If Sarah had wanted to be public about their relationship and Joline insisted her lesbianism be kept a secret from her minister father, it is hard to imagine how that would have resolved itself. One thing I noticed during the writing of this book was that—while couples differed from one another in how out they were—within the couple relationships being out was something both partners generally agreed on. I do know couples who have different levels of being out, particularly on their jobs. It isn't easy. In one couple, a professional position keeps one partner closeted while the other is able to be out. The lesbian who can be out doesn't name her partner in public. Friends and family know about their relationship. It is a delicate balance and at times creates tension in the relationship—beyond any other source of tension between them. Still, they love one another, they have consciously chosen one another. They want to live together and raise their family. They both love their work. They didn't choose the homophobic world that surrounds one partner's profession. They're doing the best they can.

Choosing. Exercising our choice to love other women means that we are pushing against all of a homophobic culture's definitions of us—definitions that tell us we are overly sexualized, dangerous, selfish creatures who are doomed to lives of unhappiness. We can choose happiness. We can choose not to be victims. We can find partners who suit us and help us grow to be our best selves.

REFERENCES

1. Judith C. Brown, "Lesbian Sexuality in Renaissance Italy: The Case of Sister Benedetta Carlini," *Signs*, Vol. IX, no. 4, pp. 751–58.

2. Pat Robertson says feminism "encourages women to leave their husbands, kill their children, practice witchcraft, destroy capitalism, and become lesbians" (quoted in *The Nation*, September 14, 1992, p. 248).

3. Suzanne Pharr, *Homophobia: A Weapon of Sexism*. Little Rock, Ark: Chardon Press, 1988.

4. Cynthia Enloe, "Heterosexist Masculinity in the Military," *Sojourner: The Women's Forum*, June, 1993, p. 2P.

5. Michelangelo Signorile, *Queer in America*. New York: Random House, 1993, p. 364.

6. Joseph P. Shapiro, "Straight Talk About Gays," *U.S. News & World Report*, July 5, 1993, pp. 42–48.

7. Kevin Fedarko, "Coming Out in the Country," *Time*, July 19, 1993, p. 35.

RESOURCES

When you need help coming out:

Mary V. Borhek, *Coming Out to Parents: A Two-Way Survival Guide for Lesbians and Gay Men and Their Parents*. Cleveland, Ohio: Pilgrim Press, 1993. A checklist for how-when-where, some arguments you may face and answers—to questions ranging from religion to HIV.

Betty Fairchild et al., *Now That You Know: What Every Parent Should Know About Homosexuality*. San Diego: Harcourt Brace Jovanovich, 1989. Give this one to them after you've done it.

ORGANIZATIONS

Federation of *Parents* and *Friends* of *Lesbians* and *Gays*, Inc. (P-FLAG or PARENTS FLAG)

P.O. Box 27605
Washington, D.C. 20038-7605
(202) 638-4200, (800) 4-FAMILY
Call or write for lists of state and local chapters.

PART FOUR

Coupling

The Couple Concept

When I began thinking about this subject and making lists and outlines of ideas I might write about, one of my lists included "becoming one-half of a couple." I was surprised at a friend's angry vehemence when she read my list. "Absolutely not," she insisted. "I'm not half of something when I join a couple. I'm not half a person, I'm not half of myself. I'm a whole person joining with another whole person."

I got it. If the language with which we name our relationships is important, so is the language that describes what those names mean to us. Growing up, I remember hearing men refer to their wives as their better halves. Usually, they were joking, and you knew they didn't mean it. "My other half" was another way of naming a spouse, as though the speaker were incomplete as an individual. The ways of talking about single women perpetuated that image—*spinster* and *old maid* were threats, not possible states of fulfilled-being.

When I came out as a lesbian, I was involved briefly with two women and then met the woman who was to be my lover for eight years. We became lovers in October, she moved into my apartment in January, and the following year we bought a house together. It never occurred to me that I wouldn't be coupled. Gay men might have multiple relationships, brag about the number of anonymous sexual partners they were with on a vacation in San Francisco, but lesbians, I was sure, lived together in couples. At least the ones I knew did. At first. Being coupled was an ideal for me and many of my peers in the early seventies. I didn't use the word *marriage* when I talked about our relationship, nor did I use it in my private thoughts. And yet I assumed I would live with her for the rest of my life.

For me, there is joy in living closely with a partner. I understand that intimacy is possible without being live-in partners, but for me there are pleasure and comfort in sharing our home. And I grow best when I am stimulated by the warmth and friction of daily intimacy. Knowing when to give and when to stand is a constant challenge, a challenge I experience most directly when I am living with a lover.

When heterosexuals form a couple bond, most often they "get married." With marriage, they create a unit called the family. When lesbians form a couple, begin living together in that configuration, we too form a family. A friend in her early thirties, who has been living with her lover for several years, returned recently from a visit to her biological family in the Midwest. "They are so unhappy," she told me, her face letting me know that this was a revelation, of sorts, to her. "I was so glad to get home. 'Thank goodness for my family here' was what I kept saying to myself." Home. Family. Those are not concepts we can let others define for us.

Family. Who is my family? I believe family is defined by function, by connection, rather than only by biological ties. I have been a supportive adult in the life of a friend's child since she was six. I'm not her aunt by blood or marriage, but I am by function and caring. "I'm trying to figure out what relationship my nephew is to my lover's son," said a lesbian in a six-year relationship. Cousins? Not automatically. When we talk about our chosen families, we are talking about consciously choosing relationships that are meaningful and healthful for us. If these lesbians were closeted, if her nieces and nephews knew nothing about the nature of her relationship to her lover, how could they begin to think of themselves as connected to her lover's child? They couldn't. Because when we speak of our "chosen family," we are, of necessity speaking about the awareness of the people involved. Chosen family isn't something that can be assigned. Do these children know one another? Do they celebrate holidays and birthdays together? Are they able to acknowledge and name the connections in the lives of the adults involved? If so, then they are cousins.

Another friend, who died recently, was the biological mother of two children and the coparent of another. The day she died, her partner's daughter's teachers came to the house after school to offer their support and condolences. This ten-year-old, raised in an openly lesbian household, introduced her teachers to her sister, her grandmother, and her aunt, and named them as such. None of these was related to her by any legal tie. Indeed, she had only recently met her comother's sister and mother; but she knew without hesitation that they were part of her family. When my friend's "family" gathered at her funeral, it included members of her biological family, her partner's biological family, a dozen or so lesbians who were her sisters-in-fact, if not legally, and other members of an extended family defined by love and caring rather than by law, sexual orientation, or biology.

In one sense, these family ties may be more tenuous than biological ones. It's tough to divorce our parents, our siblings, although some of us have been through the painful experience of being disowned by our birth families when they discovered we were lesbian. We can ignore the pain, ignore them, of course, and yet the connection is, at some level, still there. But if we ignore the ties to our chosen families, if we don't work on the relationships, the connections atrophy, disappear. And so, in another sense, the ties to our chosen families may be stronger than the automatically assumed ties to biological family. We have to pay attention to them, nurture them, or lose them.

We tend to think of a couple as an exclusive unit, and yet it means more than two people who want to join their lives. Living within the family structure of a couple defines a relationship to a wider community as well as to one another. The traditional family is patriarchal, and the right wing would like to "conserve" that tradition. Families without a patriarch call into question the male prerogative of defining and controlling our society. Lesbian families create an alternative to that power structure, even when we don't consciously think about challenging patriarchy. I didn't want to marry my lover as a challenge to anyone, but the fact of our commitment ceremony does challenge the status quo. It is small wonder the right wing wants to keep the defining of family to themselves. Joining with another woman and calling yourselves a "couple" creates a unit of strength; extending that unit through other commitments, sometimes called family ties, enhances that strength, that challenge.

Single-mother families challenge the patriarchy also, and it is interesting to compare assumptions in the language used about female-headed families in terms of poverty, welfare, irresponsibility, and sexual promiscuity. Welfare mothers—did you ever hear of a welfare father?—are usually assumed to be young black women, in spite of statistics that indicate the majority of women on welfare are white. These women may be caught in a cycle of poverty, but the commonly held assumption among the white middle class is that they could do differently—and better—if they would only change their behavior, that is, stop having children out of wedlock, get jobs, and so on. Similarly, when lesbians and gays argue that our sexual orientation is inherent and perhaps even "God-given," we are told by conservatives that we could change if we wanted to. We are given examples of homosexuals who are happily, heterosexually married and bearing and rearing children in the patriarchal family structure.

Recently, in an ironic twist, the Christian right wing has succeeded in organizing a conservative segment of the black church to lobby against the Federal Civil Rights Bill (HB 431) on the basis that it includes protection for the "immoral lifestyle" of lesbians and gays.[1] In a position paper, the Reverend C. Jay Matthews proclaims that his purpose is to "emphasize and promote the social and cultural views that are supported in the Bible," presumably those views that support patriarchy, but not those that enjoin slaves to obey their masters. As if to bolster this attempt at setting the civil rights of black people against those of lesbians and gays, *The New York Times* reported in 1993[2] that black people are rejecting the gay-rights fight as equal to their own. This was the headline, in spite of the fact that the newspaper's own poll indicated just the opposite—that 53 percent of blacks polled thought civil rights legislation for lesbians and gays was necessary, as compared to only 40 percent of white people. Homophobia and racism. Divide and conquer. My friend who is a black lesbian and grew up in one of the churches attacking homosexuals is devastated that the black church would mount such an attack on members of its own community, its own family.

Family is worth having; it is worth fighting for. Affirming that as lesbians and gays we *have* family, that we can define our own families, is not a backward strategy, not an attempt to be like the heterosexuals. It is an insistence on creating our own bases of support, on not allowing ourselves to be named outside the circle of community, on affirming our humanity. Our families will always look different from heterosexual families. That's fine. Our claiming of family is not an attempt to "blend in" with conservative forces but to transform a flawed and currently dysfunctional institution into a positive, healthful one.

If it is a given that our families will never have one daddy, one mommy, and 2.3 babies, we probably ought not to assume any other description of it either—not two mommies, not two monogamous lovers, nor any other hard and fast description of the ideal lesbian family. I lived for eight years as a single lesbian. During that time my friends were my family and gave me the daily emotional intimacy we need as human beings just to keep going. The couple I know who have been together the longest of any of my friends—approaching twenty-five years this winter—have never in all that time been monogamous. One or both has had other lovers, other relationships. They have kept separate friends as well as mutual friends. And they are in every sense life partners, who give each other primary support, who work together to shape their world into something that is life-giving, loving, expansive. When I try to imagine a description of lesbian couples, these two women and their extended family are part of that description.

All of the couples I interviewed who had children—whether from previous relationships or conceived or adopted by the couples—considered themselves to be families. Most felt connected to their partners' families and want to maintain those relationships. Deborah and

Peggy's first description of themselves to me was "We're about family." That includes more than just themselves and their children. For example, Peggy's father has always been close to his grandson Darrell, but he's also been a mentor and role model to Deborah's oldest child. Eugene was eight and Darrell was two when these "brothers" began living together. "My dad always wanted to play with Darrell," Peggy remembers, "but Darrell was a little guy. Eugene was a tough, sturdy eight-year-old, who could wrestle with Papa. Papa loved that."

Deborah laughed. "So did I. Even by the time he was eight I knew I wasn't going to be able to force him to do anything ever again. He was nearly as big as I was. He needed to know that somebody could put him in a hammerlock if he got too obnoxious." Deborah's mother lived in Florida until her death two years ago, but on her semiannual visits she stayed with Deborah and Peggy, spoiling Darrell, the family baby, just as she did Eugene and Cynthia, her own grandchildren.

When Susan went dancing with Barbara for the first time, she knew she wanted a family, specifically children. "I always felt that I'd like to have at least one child. I guess I thought it would be like a healing process for me, because of my own messed-up relationship with my parents. It was something I knew I wanted to do. I mean, I even had a crib—for years before I was able to have a baby." It was no surprise to Susan that being pregnant, the experience of having a child, made her feel more connected to Barbara and her daughter. "One thing I noticed when I was pregnant was I had this real sense of family that I never had before. I felt a sense of security, like there's always going to be a family member there. In a way, I tried to acknowledge that may not happen with him; he may grow up and not like me, his mom. He may decide to get uninvolved. But I kind of think that family connection is going to be there, and I never felt that before. That gave me a real sense of peace and security I hadn't had up to that point. The security let me open my heart to Jeanie, Barbara's daughter, in a new way." And to Barbara.

"When Susan had the baby," Barbara adds, "I thought I didn't want to be involved. I'd raised my daughter, and who needed to start this whole thing over?—you know, up all night, the earaches, the baby-sitters, the whole thing." She sighs, tired just remembering it. "But it's real hard to live with a kid and not be involved. Especially when you love his mother. Finally I said, What the hell. What does it matter if I pick him up at day care? Or give him his bath? I guess that's when I knew we were family."

For many years, family for Barbara and Susan included only them and their children. Susan's mother, from whom she'd been estranged for years, lived in rural Maine. Barbara's parents were both dead, and her one brother, a large-rig truck driver, had never married or settled down. Gradually, Susan's sister began to visit, and last year, just after Barbara's diagnosis of ovarian cancer, Susan's mother came to see her daughter and meet her seven-year-old grandson. Jeanie, Barbara's daughter, is nineteen now, but Barbara thinks a lot about what Susan's relationship with Jeanie will be if—when—Barbara dies.

Sarah and Joline don't have children, but they were practically children themselves when they first became lovers, and their families have always allowed space for their "friendship," even though it isn't stated as a family connection. The families don't know one another and probably never will, partly because the racial communities in their town are so divided, but also because the relationship isn't named and they have no other context for getting to know one another. "If there'd been a wedding or something," muses Joline, "I guess the mothers of the brides could have commiserated with one another." Sarah reminds Jo that her sisters know they are lovers and have mostly treated Sarah as extended family. "I know, I know," she agrees, "but it doesn't feel the same."

Would it be any different, I ask, if Sarah were a white man? Is "not-the-same" about race or gender? Gender, Joline answers quickly. One of her sisters is married to a white man, and both families make an effort. It isn't simple or easy, but it's an effort no one sees the need to make toward Sarah's family. Nor does Sarah's family see any connection to Joline or her family.

Seeing the connection can happen whether or not there are dependent children, of course. Seeing the connection most often results from naming the connection. When Wanda told her parents that she was moving in with Kathryn and that she considered this an important and committed relationship, they first wanted to meet Kathryn and then her parents and brothers and sisters. "I couldn't believe how open they were," Kathryn says, "and how embarrassed I was about my own family. They were appalled when I told them I was a lesbian, years ago when I was still in college, and they kept hoping I'd grow out of it. Meeting Wanda and her family wasn't part of their agenda."

Still, Kathryn hopes her parents will want to meet Wanda some-day in the not too distant future. She talks about her life with Wanda, even when her openness is met with silence. "I'm with Wanda for a long time," she smiles. "I guess I can give them time to get used to it. And I won't stop talking about it."

Naming Ourselves

We have lived together for four years. Our commitment celebration was a marriage ceremony. We share our finances, our families are merging, we have some friends in common, we no longer distinguish between "her chair" and "my sofa," and I don't know what to call her. She is my lover, best friend, life partner, confidante, spouse, buddy, housemate. She is my main squeeze. (I'm your only squeeze, she insists.) She is not my wife or my husband.

When I introduce her to people, I usually say she's my partner and let them figure out what kind of partner. Having had a couple of business partners, I know the difference, and expect others do too. I could say "life partner," but it sounds more like a prison sentence than a chosen commitment. When I say "partner" I try not to drawl like a bad imitation of an old John Wayne movie. If I were to say "spouse," I'd have to be careful not to spit. It's not a user-friendly word, *spouse*. *Long-time companion* or *loving companion* is reserved for an obituary. I long for a word with the grace and flow of *compañera* or *novia*, but they haven't found their way into English yet, and the translation of *companion* or *sweetheart* doesn't do either word justice.

Introducing my lover as my roommate or housemate or best friend may be accurate, but it is a form of concealment. Those words don't include in their definition that we are sexually linked. *Partner* is fuzzy that way. Sex isn't part of the definition, but *partner* has been used instead of *spouse* or *lover* or *wife/husband* for long enough now to *nearly* carry the connotation of sexuality. *Lover,* of course, carries the weight of sexuality and can be awkward, since heterosexual society tends to assume that being lesbian or gay is *only* about sex.

I've heard one or two women introduce one another as wife. I can't get there. I know it was important to me to reclaim the word *marriage*— meaning a spiritual, social, and sexual bond—for the relationship I was forming with my lover. There is no other word in English that expresses the totality of that union, and so in spite of the fact that "marriage" is what heterosexuals do, I want to be able to do it too. I don't have, personally, the same feelings about the word *wife*, or even *husband.* A wife, historically, was a piece of property. A wife was owned by a husband, or a man, and I have a hard time finding any-thing about that concept that I want to reclaim. A wife does the cook-ing and cleaning and child care. The term is bound by historical social restrictions that limit it. I think if I referred to my partner as "my wife" in public two things would happen: she'd be furious and I couldn't say it without starting to giggle.

So what do we do? I've settled on *lover* or *partner*, depending on the circumstances, until the language produces something more lovely. I'm in fairly good company with this. A 1988 survey (Partners: Task Force for Gay & Lesbian Couples) found that 35 percent of the lesbians surveyed used the word *partner* and 30 percent used *lover.*[3]

Does it matter? That's the other question I've heard raised over and over when issues about language are brought up. Trust me, it matters. Language shapes our thinking, and how we think about our relationships shapes what they become. If we expect them to be tran-sient, not permanent, if we expect them to be a peripheral part of our lives, they will be that. Calling the woman with whom you share the most intimate and profound part of your life your *roommate* trivializes the relationship. My father knew that, even before I had named myself a lesbian to him. My lover of several years went with me to my mother's funeral. My mother's sister, whom I hadn't seen in many years, was introduced to my lover and commented, "Oh, you're the roommate." "Oh, no," my father insisted to my surprise. "She's much more than that. They own a *house* together." I didn't know whether to laugh or cry. He knew instinctively her importance to me, but he didn't have the words and I hadn't given him the permission.

A year later, when he was visiting us at Christmas, we were driving down the road to a neighbor's party, my lover and I bemoaning the event and the necessity. "Oh, cheer up," he told us. "Maybe you'll meet your future husbands there." My lover nearly drove the car into a ditch, and I decided I was going to have to say the word *lesbian* out loud to my father. If I didn't say it, I could hardly criticize him for trivializing our relationship, although my impulse was to accuse him furiously of just that. "You'd never suggest my sister have an affair outside of her marriage," I wanted to say to him, "so how could you suggest I might want another relationship than this one?"

After that day, my father, and later his wife, spoke of my partner as my partner. She and her children became members of our family. Their support was part of a network of friends and family who recognized our relationship and helped us affirm its centrality to our lives. They could give us this support because they had the words to name our relationship and they had our permission to use them.

Setting Boundaries

The codependency tango. The lesbian meltdown. Merger madness. We all know the scene. If we haven't lived it personally, well, we've seen our friends do it. It's so much easier to see in other couples, isn't it? "When Sue and Jill got together, they became one personality and it was Jill's." Is there any greater condemnation? Does this really happen to lesbian couples? Why? Can we prevent it?

I asked my couples about this, the long-established ones and the newer couples, the older and the younger, and everyone knew what I was talking about. "It's a little bit like the myth of lesbian bed-death in the third month of every relationship," Leslie assured me. "Sure it happens, but we worry about it more than it actually happens." So, I wondered, if we stop talking about it, will it go away? "No, not exactly." Leslie shrugged. "I just don't think it's that big a deal. How do you separate what's good, healthy sharing from sick codependency?"

That is another way of posing the question. Jan and I have talked or laughed about this issue. Some of her coworkers think it is outrageous that I make Jan's lunch for her most mornings. We think they're jealous, they say we're codependent. I like making her lunch. I love that I get to stay home and work at my computer while she trucks off to the office. Sending her with a lunch she'd like to eat is cost effective, and we both enjoy it. I don't compromise myself or my boundaries by making her lunch. When I'm traveling, or busy in other ways, she is perfectly capable of making her own lunch, and willing to do so. I experience one of life's small but important pleasures whenever I open my dresser drawer and find clothes I threw in the laundry three days ago washed and neatly folded. These are not boundary issues for us, but some of the joys of being coupled.

If I still have to do everything for myself, maintain my own way of doing every daily chore, buy my own tickets for every concert, and go to bed whenever I feel like it, regardless of what my partner wants or is doing, what is the point of coupling? On the other hand, if I can't buy a new shirt without her approval, if I wait for her to go to bed when I'm truly exhausted and need to sleep, if I won't express an opinion that differs from hers, then I am having boundary difficulties.

These difficulties seem to be the most harmful when couples don't know they are happening. Boundary issues sneak up on us when we aren't looking, when we're feeling warm and fuzzy and loving. What could be wrong about wanting her to be a part of your life? Plenty. In my first relationship, my partner finally blew up when I agreed for about the fourth time to have dinner with friends—agreed for both of us without asking her. She made me go to dinner alone, and it was the last time I scheduled her into my life without consulting her. I had not realized I was usurping her space, violating her boundaries, her right to make her own decisions about her time.

When Jan and I began living together, we had both lived with several other partners. From those experiences, we both knew about boundary issues, and I knew that one problem for me was time and scheduling. Sure enough, about the third day we were cohabiting, Jan changed her schedule around in order to be home for dinner. I had planned to go to a meeting, not realizing that in complaining earlier that day on the phone about her schedule I had—she thought—asked her to come home early. As I got ready to leave, she sat stony-faced and uncommunicative on the couch. I hesitated at the door. If I went to the meeting, wouldn't I be keeping my boundaries intact? Right. But if I went to the meeting, I knew there was a chance she wouldn't be there when I got back. I took off my jacket and went and sat next to her. We began to talk. I missed the meeting, but it hadn't been very important, except as a symbol; and we didn't need that particular symbol anymore.

When Ann and Margaret found themselves fighting about what color tile to install in Ann's bathroom, they were experiencing a boundary issue. Leslie and Daphne keep their financial lives separate because they don't want to have a boundary issue around whose money is whose. Lisa and Mariana have said they're glad they aren't both actors or both writers, because keeping their successes and failures separate might be too hard, and they already have trouble in this area.

Having separate friends is important to all three of these couples. "Hers, mine, and ours," says Lisa. "Not that I don't like her friends, but having friends who reflect our professional and personal interests is important to our sense of self." Wow, I think. That sounds like Lisa learned it somewhere. I wonder how it works. Lisa shrugs. "Theater people are different, you know? I need to hang out with them. Mariana doesn't need to hang out with theater people. She needs to know writers." Does Mariana have writer friends? "Some," she agrees. "But it's not as important to me as it is to Lisa. Everybody thinks they can write. I meet writers at the temp agency, I meet them when I go to the gym to work out, they're on our softball team." "But you do have your writers' group," protests Lisa. "It's not all that different."

I leave Lisa and Mariana to argue the point. My interest is more along the lines of personal friendships, those deep and lasting intimacies that probably existed before we became lovers with our current partners and may outlast any partner relationship. Those intimacies are sometimes perceived by a lover as threatening, and sometimes giving up such a friendship can be used as a bargaining chip in a boundary war.

"Oh," Daphne recognizes what I mean. "Sheila." Sheila? "I couldn't have even a phone conversation with Becky if Sheila knew about it. Becky," she explains, "was my best friend back East, while I was in college and during my first job. She's still my best friend, actually—best friend, that is, who's not a lover." I nod, accepting the distinction. "I knew Sheila was jealous from the very beginning of our relationship. I sort of didn't call Becky right away. I mean, she knew I'd moved in with Sheila, but I waited to give her the phone number. I called her one night when Sheila was watching television, and that wasn't a success." I guess that Sheila had gotten angry and Daphne nods. "We didn't get to bed until three in the morning." She pauses reflectively. "I didn't deal with it up front. I knew I should have. But I just made a point of talking to Becky from work. I could do that every now and then. One of the things we talked about was how wrong it was that she couldn't call me at my home." Did Sheila think Daphne was no longer in contact with Becky? "That's what I told her," she admits shamefacedly. "It's not something I'm proud of, not something I'd ever do again. I wouldn't be with Leslie now if it weren't okay for us to have separate friends."

"Boundaries? Boundaries?" Sandra's voice slid up a couple of notches as she considered the question. "I live with seven kids and you ask me about boundaries between me and Beth? Get serious."

"Oh, come on," I pushed. "I know you had to fight to get time alone together in your day—that's what mommies' hour after dinner was a response to—but surely there's something that you two had to negotiate?"

"Actually, maybe," Beth admits, taking over the conversation. She has been watching carefully to see what I've been saying. "Let's face it, we're both mothers and we're both caretakers. I know those two don't always go together, but for us they do. I try to relate to people by taking care of them. Most times they let me, too," she added, a little ruefully. "But I never met somebody who did it exactly the same way I do it until I met Sandra. Have you ever seen a caretaker try to take care of another caretaker?" I allow as to how I probably have not.

"It's not bad, actually," Sandra insists. "When I was taking care of my husband and the three kids, no one was taking care of me. Now I take care of Beth and seven kids, but she's there taking care of them too, and . . ." she paused for emphasis, "she's taking care of me. That's new. Totally new."

As we talk, I realize that what Sandra and Beth are describing is liberating, not restricting. Each has found a partner who is as responsible (or overly responsible, depending on who's watching) as she herself is. When Sandra says she'll do the shopping on the way home, Beth knows it will happen and she won't have to guess what else to have for dinner when someone "forgets" or is too busy to carry through. When Beth says she'll pick up the kids at day care, Sandra doesn't have to plan her day at school so that if a call comes, saying, "I got tied up at the office, honey," she'll be free to dash to day care. When Beth says she'll pick them up, she picks them up, which means that Sandra can settle in and get her lesson plan for the next day finished before she goes home.

"It is kind of amazing to me," Sandra agrees. "I was so used to doing it all myself, having the kids be my responsibility, and even when I thought my husband and I had agreed to share a responsibility, ultimately he was only helping out. The real deal was that it was mine."

Obviously, boundaries were an issue for both of these women in their marriages, and they haven't really learned how to set boundaries any better than before. "I chose better this time," Beth suggests. "Surely that's an indication I learned something, isn't it?" But she's laughing, and I can see that because her relationship with Sandra works for her, she isn't really very interested in a theoretical model of relationships that would work with someone else.

When Susan talked about boundaries with her lover, Barbara, her conversation included a "before and after." Before and after Barbara's diagnosis with ovarian cancer. "We had a lot of issues in the beginning," Susan admits, "particularly around me having the baby and how much Barbara would be involved. But it's kind of hard to remember that now. Most days I feel like I don't have any boundaries. Whatever she needs is what I want to do. It's no different from having a sick child." She shrugs and looks tired. Barbara was sleeping in the next room, mute testimony to the reality that life sometimes won't conform to idealized structures of mutuality and independence.

Boundaries, basically, are what we talk about when we don't have them, when they aren't working, or when they're working so well we can't get close to anyone, especially that one person we most want to be close with. Boundaries are fluid and can expand or contract to meet different needs at different times. When Barbara was holding her boundaries rigidly so that she wouldn't get absorbed into Susan's child-rearing needs, Susan responded by taking care of her own life, her own needs. She felt less drawn to Barbara at that time, less intimate with her, but then she was establishing a relationship with her new son. Gradually, as Barbara's boundaries over the child-care issue relaxed, Susan let herself become less guarded, and both women say that at this time in their relationship they felt very happy with one another and the intimacy between them. Now Barbara's needs are defined by her illness and imminent death. Susan knows this period in her life is finite, and she needs to be as open and available to Barbara as she has the strength to be. She has very little energy left for herself or her son, but she has arranged for friends to help out with some extra treats, visits, and overnights for Darien. Herself? There will be time for that, she says, in the near future.

Creating Rituals

Early on in our relationship, Jan and I began doing things that we found amusing or comforting; sometimes we would remember the words or the action and repeat it, ritualizing the moment as a part of our intimacy. One night when we were both reading in bed, Jan turned out her light first, turned to me, and asked petulantly, "You gonna read all night?" "Yup," I answered, stroking her cheek. And I did read a few more pages that night before my eyelids drooped irretrievably. The next night she finished reading first again and asked again, "You gonna read all night?" "Yup," I said again. "You gonna turn the pages real noisy like you did last night and keep me awake?" I raised one eyebrow and tried to keep reading. "Yup," I answered, and then we both started to giggle like teenagers. Now the question is the same, no matter who turns the light out first. It isn't a real question anymore, if it ever was; it is a part of our ritual about going to bed.

What is it about, this ritual? Our comfort level with one another. Our ability to tease and be teased without taking offense. And like every ritual, it is a way of expressing our belonging—at this place, at this time, we belong here, together.

Rituals define our days together, our living place together, our playtime together. None of them were consciously created, but we have been conscious about their place and function in our life. We value them. We find it difficult when they are interrupted by visiting company or one of us traveling away from home. But even in that difficulty, we are affirming our life as a couple, our mutuality, as we miss our shared rituals.

Rituals can develop spontaneously or we can plan them. Making time after dinner for a quiet conversation about their days—that's a ritual Beth and Sandra developed after a few months of frazzled inability to connect with one another. "We had spent more time together, alone together, when we were living separately," says Beth, "and we knew that we needed the intimacy that comes out of that. Falling into bed at midnight, too exhausted to talk at all, just wasn't cutting it."

Sandra agrees and explains that they were getting short, irritable with one another and their children. "We called a time out one weekend. Beth's kids were with their father and we got a baby-sitter for the rest. We went to a coffeehouse where no one knew us and the phone wouldn't ring for us. We talked nonstop for four hours. It was wonderful." Now Sandra and Beth leave the dishes to whomever and go upstairs to their private place for an hour after dinner. The children adjusted fairly easily. "We'd like to think that harmony reigns down there while we're upstairs," Sandra admits ruefully. "You know, that everyone is doing their chores, getting to their homework. But what they're doing really doesn't matter as long as we don't have to be part of it for that one hour."

Lisa and Mariana had to work out a ritual around going to sleep. They hadn't lived together when they first became lovers because they were in college, living in separate dorm rooms. When they graduated and decided to live together in New York, both were excited about the arrangement. "Then we found out we kept very different schedules," says Mariana. "The kind of thing you sort of vaguely know when you're lovers, but don't have to deal with. I mean I knew never to call her before noon if I wanted to talk coherently with her. I didn't think about what that meant at the other end. That she didn't like to go to sleep before two or three in the morning." Nights, late nights, are Lisa's most creative times. Mornings belong to Mariana. "At first I felt really pissed when she wouldn't come to bed with me," Mariana continues. "I tried staying up with her a few nights, but that didn't work. I'm impossible after eleven and at midnight I cease to function altogether. Then I realized I liked the alone time in the morning. Even if we were both going to work at 8, I'd get up at 5:30 and write. Lisa'd roll out of bed about 7:45."

How did it work out? I asked. What made it okay? "I figured out that I needed not to be ignored. If I was going to bed I wanted her to miss me, even if she was going to be glad to have the time to herself. So, basically, we just make a point of saying a long goodnight to one another." I suspect there is a bit more to this ritual and wait expectantly. Mariana looks a little embarrassed, and then confesses. "Actually, she begs me to stay up with her and I beg her to come to bed with me. Then I go to bed and she stays up. It sounds a little silly, I know . . . " She shrugs. But it works, I add silently. And nothing that works is really that silly.

"Oh, God, rituals," Leslie says disdainfully. "Rituals? We try never to do anything the same way twice. I mean, who wants to be bored?" Surely some things happen the same way, I insist. Isn't repetition nice sometimes? Leslie is shaking her head no, then remembers. "Well, one thing you can count on happening the same is that after we've had sex, no matter when it is, what time of day or night, the minute it's over, Daphne turns into Chatty Cathy." Daphne is present and starts to laugh. Leslie watches her for a moment, as though she doesn't see anything to laugh about, and then she starts to laugh too. "Chatty Cathy?" I ask, not sure if I'm allowed to laugh.

"Sure, you know," Daphne gulps between giggles, "the doll that talks. Chatty Cathy." I'm still not getting it, so she becomes serious long enough to explain. "Leslie is serious about sex and afterward she's really profound. You know, moved. Quiet. Kind of introverted. Me? I'm turned on in a different way. I want to cuddle and talk. Just yammer, really. It's my way of coming down."

So how is this a ritual? Leslie shrugs. "Maybe it's not," she says. "It's just that I would think I was in bed with the wrong person if she didn't start to chat. I've gotten kind of used to it." And I can tell from her tone of affection that she has, and that it is something she might miss if Daphne changed.

For two years, during my life as a "single" lesbian, I had a lover who lived two thousand miles away. We both traveled a lot at that time, so managed to see one another nearly once a month. The most difficult part of the relationship was coming together again, remembering who we were together, and picking up the intimacy where we had left it. I know couples for whom this is not a problem, but for me it was nearly impossible. In retrospect, I wonder if we couldn't have created a ritual to help us with this transition.

Ann and Margaret don't see one another once a month, but they are together for longer periods than a weekend, since Ann doesn't work anymore and Margaret is basically self-employed. The hardest part, they both agree, is being the one who is visited, rather than the visitor. "If you get out of your own life by going someplace else," Margaret explains, "it's easier to relax, have fun, not worry about what else ought to be going on. But when you're in your own day-to-day life, trying to be relaxed and take care of business at the same time, I can tell you it gets confusing."

How do they manage their coming together, I ask, remembering my own inability to maintain a long-distance relationship. "It works best if the one who is being visited sets aside some time," Ann tells me. "That may seem obvious, but when I'd go down to Margaret's home in Mérida, there'd always be something I just had to see or some adventure she'd decided we had to go off on. And since she's a travel agent, it usually involved other people." So what they've worked out is a kind of ritual, a way of structuring their first hours together that allows them the space to reconnect. Their rules are simple: no travel, no other people, some food. "We both like to eat," Margaret said, laughing. "And according to my mother, no good ritual ever went without food." Does the ritual include sex? "Not always, but usually," Ann smiles at the question. "I'm not a kid anymore. I'll usually choose food and sleep before sex. But when the basics are taken care of . . ." She leaves the thought dangling, and I can see that Margaret is nodding as if she'd figured out how to take care of the basics very early in the day.

Things We Do Together,
Things We Do Apart

What draws a couple together? What makes your lover the woman you want to be partnered with? What does that mean to you? Do you love the same leisure-time activities? Do you do the same work? Is your bond about children? Are you both nuts about your cats? or your motorcycles? or your collection of Mickey Mouse memorabilia?

No matter how well suited we feel to the woman we're partnered with, there will be things one woman needs in her life that the other could live without easily. Sometimes these differences are insignificant, and sometimes they are about the most important things in our lives. Two stand out for many of the couples I talked with: spirituality and politics.

"We have a very obvious difference, if you're talking about religion," says Beth. "I'm Jewish and Sandra's not." Sandra sighs with mock despair. "Go ahead, say it. I'm a WASP—the original white Anglo-Saxon Protestant, that's me. I'm even upper middle class. That was more of a religion than the occasional church service we attended when someone my father knew got married or died."

But spirituality is different from religion and we all know what I *mean* but finding the words is difficult. "It's important to me that my children know they're Jewish, and that they know what that means, both in a historical sense and a spiritual sense." Beth pauses. "So I guess in that way that part of my spiritual life is separate from Sandra. It's me and the kids. And sometimes their father. And usually their grandparents. But it doesn't seem like the most important part."

What would the most important part be? They're quiet for a moment. Then Sandra answers. "The first time we ever made love—I mean really made love with all the time we needed and privacy—I've never felt so profoundly moved in my life." She leans forward, her hands tracing an urgent pattern in the air. "I wanted to shout hallelujah or something like that. I was exhilarated. If I'd never known I had a soul before, I knew it then." She stops and sits back. "I cried. I just lay there and cried for the woman I'd been who'd never been able to feel anything like that before." Beth reaches over and takes Sandra's hand. "That's the part of our spiritual life we share," she tells me. "And it's more important than I ever imagined it could be." Sandra nods her agreement. "Obviously," she says, laughing, "that part of our spiritual life is something we do together."

Sandra and Beth don't feel that having separate institutional religious experiences is an issue for them. They respect one another's traditions. And they do important holidays as a family—Yom Kippur and Passover with Beth's parents, Christmas-Santa for all the children in their own home. "If Christianity were more important to me," says Sandra, "it might have been an issue, but we've never had to argue about where we'd spend a holiday or which ones we'd celebrate with which family."

Other women found these issues harder to negotiate. Marty, the ex-nun, says that one of the discomforts in her relationship with Joan was that, at the very bedrock, Joan didn't respect Marty's attachment to her community of faith. It took some time for Marty to understand that, however. "For a lot of years, our political life was our spiritual life," remembers Marty. "Or at least it felt like that to me. In the early years of feminism, I *felt* like when I was first in the convent. We had the same sense of enthusiasm, of being dedicated to our cause, of making life better for a lot of people. And it was about community, too. That's what spirituality is to me, really. That's what church means, in its best sense, a community of people engaged in making the world more just."

Marty explains that when she and Joan became more isolated in their life, partly because of their drinking, partly because their feminist community was changing, she looked to her church again for a spiritual community. "Joan freaked. To her, the church was patriarchy and she couldn't see anything good or useful coming from it." Much later, when it was too late for the relationship, Marty and Joan both found another kind of spiritual-community support in twelve-step recovery groups. But Marty will always be attached to the church, no matter what else she finds in her life. "I was born into it," she explains. "You don't cease to be your parents' child just because you grow up, grow away from them. That's the way I feel about the church. I hope the next time I have a relationship it will be with a woman who understands that part of me. Or at least won't hate that part of me."

Peggy and Deborah both attend the local Zion African Methodist Church. As it was for Marty, the church was something they grew up with, a part of their community, their self-definition. Joline, whose father was the Baptist minister, doesn't go to church often, and while Sarah and Joline don't share a spiritual community, they feel that their spiritual values are very similar. Margaret, who is Jewish, misses that feeling of "likeness" in her relationship with Ann. Rachel, her longtime partner, who died a few years ago, was Jewish, and Margaret liked not having to explain an important part of herself to her lover. "But that's more about family than about spirituality for me," she explains. "Ann and I do have some of the same spirituality. We both find ourselves most open that way when we're out in the mountains— in nature somewhere—and where there aren't any people to speak of."

As with spirituality, a definition of politics often depends on who is making it. Marty and Joan considered themselves a good match politically because of their involvement in feminism and community organizing. Peggy and Deborah don't have much to say about feminism; their politics expresses itself in their work with the NAACP.

Beth and Sandra agree that they are living their politics, being out as a lesbian couple with seven children whenever and wherever they can.

"I paid my dues," says Margaret. "I'm sixty years old and I put in a lot of time. Now the younger ones have to do the politics. Which is a good thing," she says, laughing, "since I could never get Ann to go to a meeting of any kind." Ann, who is sixty-seven, never thought of herself as "political." For her as a lesbian, "it was just a question of making a little elbow room so I could live my life." If Margaret wanted to do some political work today, Ann says she wouldn't mind, but it's not something she's interested in for herself.

Wanda and Kathryn, a fairly new couple in their early thirties, are more concerned about their political differences. "I come from a family of Jewish liberals. If you weren't active, at least you gave money to the right causes," Wanda says. "But Kathryn's family . . . well, they didn't even vote. They thought politics was stupid. And something they couldn't control or affect, so they didn't even try."

Is that affecting Kathryn and Wanda's relationship today? "I think so," Wanda muses slowly. "It's about what we want to do in our free time. I joined the collective at the women's bookstore last year. It's not very big, but we function as a kind of community center. Then I volunteer for the AIDS hotline one night a week. I think feminism is important, *still* is important, you know," she laughs and shrugs, "and so are gay and lesbian politics."

What is Kathryn's perspective on this? "Feminism isn't about politics for me," she says urgently, and I can tell she doesn't want to be misunderstood or misrepresented. "Feminism is an attitude, a bedrock. But it's not something I have to do. It's one of the givens. I don't understand why you have to spend time on it. It's not how I want to spend my time away from work."

The tension between Wanda and Kathryn hasn't become too difficult for them. They talk about what they want for their life together and try to withhold judgment about one way's being "better" than the other. If they can work out ways for each of them to fulfill their sense of what is important in this sensitive arena, if they can give each other space to express their differences, their relationship can benefit. "I fell in love with Wanda because of some of the things she was doing, some of the things she believed," says Kathryn slowly. "I admire them, but they aren't how I do it. I don't think we have to become the same just to be a couple."

Kathryn is right. Our differences don't separate us when we respect them: they are the excitement of the unknown, the suspense of learning someone who is not exactly like us. There is no aspect of a relationship that we absolutely have to do together. Each couple will find those areas that join them and those areas that allow them to be special, unique, and exciting to one another.

Changing Midstream
Without Getting Thrown

*I*t's inevitable. The habits and routines that comfort us at one stage of a relationship lose their charm. Our jobs or careers change, our life direction changes, some personal habit changes. The doctor says you have to exercise and change your diet. What happens to that quiet morning time with your lover over coffee and donuts every day? Or you decide you really will get up early and write that book or article you've been talking about for years. Your lover nods fondly. Until your changes affect her. She can't stand hearing the alarm go off at 5 A.M. You decide to sleep in the spare bedroom three nights a week to accommodate both of you. She is furious. Are you saying that sleeping with her is no longer important? You're hurt and angry. I thought you really wanted me to do this writing, you accuse, but you're not supporting me in it.

Sometimes we slide into changes and barely notice them. Both of our jobs keep us later during a busy summer, and dinner becomes less of a shared time. We substitute, without ever talking about it, meeting for popcorn and talking about our days while the late news is on. Generally, these are the changes that don't threaten a relationship, at least not at first. They don't readjust the basic terms of the relationship. Other changes do.

"I'm a workaholic," Deborah admits. "I need to be busy, whether it's on my job or taking the kids to Scouts or volunteering for the NAACP dinner committee, I like to be doing things. When Peg and I first got together, we were pretty even in that. She had work and her weight lifting and her son *and* she was in school, finishing her master's." She laughs. "Sometimes I wonder when we had time to get together." But it became more of an issue in the third year of their relationship, when Peg finished her degree and began to be free in the evenings and more free on the weekends.

"I wanted Deborah to be around more. It was okay to go our separate ways so much when we didn't have a choice, but when I finished school, I figured we had a chance to decide—did we want to do this thing together or not? Mostly I heard her saying not. That got me."

How much time we spend together as a couple is a major issue in a relationship, and changing that basic agreement can knock us off track. Deborah and Peggy recognized that and began to look for ways to accommodate. But the adjustment they eventually made to this change created an even more significant change, one they had not counted on. "We began to do some things together," Deborah remembers. "I was working on the NAACP dinner, and when that was over they asked me to be chair of planning for the next year. Peg helped me out some with that, kind of behind the scenes. Then she got interested and started taking over the entertainment part of the dinner. I was doing the awards for community work and she was planning the entertainment . . . " She paused. "That sounds great to me," I said. "Was it a problem?" She laughs. "Well, let me put it this way. Some people started figuring out we lived together, that we were *together*, and it made them uncomfortable, and they made us uncomfortable."

Changing how out we are in our communities is a major, major adjustment. We can't do it unilaterally. If Deborah had been willing to say, "Yes, she's my lover, get over it," and Peg had not wanted to be known as a lesbian in that community, they would have had a lot more to deal with. As it was, they still had trouble. "In the end," Peg tells me, "we just decided to ignore the innuendoes. We were both comfortable with that. We never denied anything and we never confirmed anything. Let 'em wonder, was what I said." "And, you know," Deborah adds, "they got over it. Now everybody in the organization knows we share a home, and they treat us like a couple."

By the time Deborah and Peggy finished dealing with the fallout of being more out in their community, the issue about how much time they would spend together had resolved itself. "We work on some projects together now," says Peg, "and we make sure we get at least one evening on the weekend that's just for us at home." Other than that, they each define their own participation in community and social events.

How much time? Which evenings? Weekends? Whether a couple is living together or separately, these are questions that have to be answered. For Jan and me, time alone has recently become an issue. I have lots of it. I work at home while she goes off to a school and office. She comes home and I am glad to see her, ready for companionship and conversation. But she hasn't had a moment to herself all day, and that is hard for her. She wants some time in our home when she is alone, when the space is all hers, and she can do something or nothing, but she is alone. How does this make me feel? I could be hurt and rejected, but I know how I would be if the circumstances were reversed. I *need* time alone, time to think, to wander around the house, to stare at the wall. Whatever. And so we are finding ways for both of us to have the time we need. It's worth negotiating, since we come back from our time alone ready to be together again.

There is no one right way to be sure that the changes we need to make will enhance our relationship rather than diminish or destroy it. But if we are conscious that we are changing and that some adjustments may be necessary, we are far less likely to experience the slam of hitting a brick wall when our partner says, "You want to what?"

Kathryn and Wanda have gone into therapy to discuss the changes they are contemplating. "Why not?" Wanda asks defensively. "Look at what we're doing—moving in together, moving to a new community, and living on one salary (Kathryn's) instead of two." Enough change, and the accompanying stress, I agree, to derail any relationship. Still, these are changes that they have both agreed on, that will affect them both. The details they need to work out are structural, but the structures will affect their emotional lives. Did the therapy help? I want to know. "We'd like to know, too," admits Kathryn. "The changes are still pretty much in the future. I feel good we're being more conscious of them. I think that's what matters in the long run."

When Marty and Joan had been living together for three years, it became obvious that the bed-and-breakfast Joan was running was a full-time job for two during the peak seasons. Marty was tired of teaching, tired of being closeted in her job, and began to think about quitting teaching and starting a counseling practice—with an office in their home—that would allow her to help with the bed-and-breakfast, as necessary, while also augmenting her income. Joan admitted that she'd been very nervous when Marty first began to talk about quitting her job. "I'd always figured we'd have that income to fall back on if the bed-and-breakfast went belly up. Now she was talking about having two businesses that might go bad."

Joan and Marty belonged to a women's support group. "This was the late seventies," Joan remembers, "and our support group was pretty central to our lives. We weren't doing consciousness raising so much anymore, but we were meeting once a month to keep one another on track, talk about the feminist issues we were reading about, that kind of thing."

Economic issues were an important topic in the group, and Joan and Marty brought Joan's discomfort with Marty's quitting her job to the group for discussion. "The group suggested the obvious, but it was a help at the time, to have women say my fears were important. They pointed out that either of us could go back to work temporarily if the businesses didn't work. But what helped us the most was when one of the women asked what it was going to be like for both of us to be working at home. Wow. That stopped me cold. I mean, I was used to working on my own, setting my own schedule, with no one looking over my shoulder. Now here was Marty suggesting she help me *and* be in the house all day doing her thing." She pauses, shaking her head at the memory. "I don't think we would have survived the transition if they hadn't said we needed to have some ground rules for how to handle it."

What kind of ground rules? "At first we were pretty rigid. We wanted it to be like it had been—not seeing each other until the workday was over. And some of that was necessary, since Marty's clients needed privacy, a sense that this office was a separate space. But gradually we mellowed. We'd have lunch together, or if she wasn't booked for the afternoon, we'd go shopping for the bed-and-breakfast groceries together." Marty started her practice during the spring while she was still teaching and when there weren't too many guests coming to stay, but by summer Joan needed her assistance in the morning when they were preparing breakfasts. And it took two of them to clean, shop, prepare for new guests. Marty kept her client schedule low during the summer and let it build up during the fall and winter, which seemed like part of the natural flow of her business anyway. Guidelines for how to manage the transition became a natural part of how they did business together.

Consciousness or awareness that the change will have an impact is the key here. Ground rules or guidelines for how to handle transitions don't have to be complicated; they do need to recognize what it is that's going to be different and give each partner time to adjust, to flex, to find a comfortable place in the new pattern. A new job, a new schedule, a new health consideration (yours, hers, or another family member's), a loss of anything we're accustomed to, these things cause stress along the fault lines of our lives. Guidelines can be like the rope a rock climber throws out: you may never need it, but knowing it is there can save you a lot of worry.

REFERENCES

1. Rev. C. Jay Matthews, "The Black Church Position Statement on Homosexuality," *The Call and Post*, Cleveland, Ohio, June 10, p. 5c.

2. *The New York Times*, June 28, 1993.

3. Partners: Task Force for Gay & Lesbian Couples, "Summary of Results of Partners' National Survey of Lesbian & Gay Couples," Box 9685, Seattle, WA 98109-0685.

RESOURCES

Two books by lesbians who are therapists about how we can make our relationships work and last:

Betty Berzon, *Permanent Partners: Building Gay and Lesbian Relationships That Last*. New York: E. P. Dutton, 1988.

D. Merilee Clunis and G. Dorsey Green, *Lesbian Couples*. Seattle, Washington: Seal Press, 2nd ed. 1993.

PART FIVE

Living Together

Making a Home
for Ourselves

For me, there is joy in living closely with a partner. I understand that intimacy is possible without being live-in partners, but I find pleasure and comfort in sharing our home. And I grow best when I am stimulated by the warmth and friction of daily intimacy. Knowing when to give and when to stand is a constant challenge, a challenge I experience most directly when I am living with a lover. Whatever forces are ranged against us in the world—and there are many—facing them with her seems less overwhelming than facing them alone. Facing life with her reminds me about what is important and what is not, reminds me that I had best live today and not wait for some better day to come along.

When we talk about intimacy and only mean sex, I think we are missing some essential ingredients. Sex can be a part of intimacy, but it need not be; and surely sex can happen without intimacy. In my life, intimacy is about being paid attention to—profound, deep attention—and giving the same to another person. Intimacy is also about caring for and being cared for, about dailiness—the repetition of small acts that create and express love.

So we're in love. We're going to do it: move in together. This isn't a casual affair. We want our lives to be more joined. What's the next step? Is it different for us than for any of those other couples, those heterosexuals who fall in love?

Yes, in a word. If we're renting, we have to find a landlord who will accept two women with lots of women friends, something that is easier today than it might have been in years past, and always something that is easier than if we were two men together, according to my gay male friends. When Jan and I moved to Arizona and wanted to rent an apartment, our cat and dog presented greater obstacles than our relationship.

But then we have to find a neighborhood to live in where we won't be too vulnerable, too visible, too awkwardly different. How can we know that? A walk around the block, keeping an eye out for people like us? Recommendations from friends? Follow our gut instinct, the vibes of a place? All of the above, believe me, and anything else we can think of to be safe, or at least live with the illusion of safety.

When I moved with a lover to an isolated farm on a dirt road in upstate New York, we knew the isolation was double-edged: not as many people would know our business and at the same time we were essentially unprotected. In a poem I wrote about that time and place, I remembered "no locks on our doors but we own/one splitting ax three butchering knives/a sledgehammer a chainsaw and a rifle/tools of necessity."[1] I lied about the rifle; it seemed like a good idea at the time, in that place, not to admit we didn't have one.

But basically, I felt safe in that home, even though, toward the end of our years there, a neighbor's son who knew we were lesbian began to drive by with his friends and taunt us, screaming epithets, blowing up our mailbox with an explosive. Safety is always an imaginary construct, an essentially creative act that allows us to go on living and do our work and love our families. We do the concrete things we can do to defend ourselves and those we love, and after that . . . . If we live paranoid, then we are defeated, not only by the forces outside of us but also by our own internalized fears.

Home means something slightly different to each of us, and the woman who finds a lover whose definition of home matches hers in some essential ways is very lucky indeed. Over the years, I've observed the lives of my friends, my potential lovers, and even my occasional lovers, and very few of them are living in homes that would be "just right" for me. I couldn't live with my ex-lover and her new lover, nor with my lover and her sister, nor in a collective household—as some of my friends do. I do not, at this point in my life, want to live with a lover who has small children. I would not willingly choose to live with a lover who never picked up her clothes or wet towels, nor, conversely, with a lover who needed an immaculate, dustless home. I assume my life looks the same to many others. Not quite "just right" for them.

Making a Match
with Your Mate

When I went to Jan's home for the first time, I saw that we had fairly similar tastes in furnishing, decorating, and levels of cleanliness. Using the sink in her bathroom didn't horrify me, nor did I feel the need to wipe it down carefully, checking the mirror for spots, each time I used it. She kept the house vacuumed "well enough" for me, and the door to her seventeen-year-old son's room was usually closed—that territory was no longer her responsibility. I saw all of this after we had become lovers but well before we decided to merge our households. And she had seen enough of how I lived to have a similar level of confidence that we could live together without *that* being an area of stress.

When we first moved in together, she gave up her more expensive apartment (her son was leaving for college) and moved into that small space I had thought would fit only one. I remembered how smug I'd felt, making a statement to potential lovers—by my choice of a space that would suit only one person—about how I intended to live alone. Jan hadn't missed the statement, she just ignored it.

We were able to live in small quarters for seven months because we knew before we began that we wanted to move—not just to a new house but to a new landscape. The bedroom we shared was so small we had to turn sideways to get out of bed. We put some of her furniture in the living room and some of her dishes in the kitchen. Some of both of our belongings got tossed or sold in a garage sale. Things weren't that important to either of us, and they still aren't. Space is. How much space, how it looks, how it can be used, who shares it. We must have been in love. For two people to whom space is so important to share one tiny bedroom, one kitchen, one bathroom, one small living room, and one study—that's pretty impressive.

The only other time I've lived with a woman, it happened similarly. I had a small apartment. She left her home and came to live in mine. For nearly a year it was fine. Our desks were side by side in the small office. The cats could choose which typewriter to try to sit on top of. We shared every inch of space. After a year we bought a house and began to renovate it. At first we had two rooms: a kitchen downstairs and a bedroom upstairs. The two desks went in the bedroom, side by side. Gradually we renovated other rooms, and finally there were two studies, a guest room, a large living room, a family room off the kitchen, and—at last—a large office and garage connected by a breezeway to the house. When things were well with us, two rooms had been plenty of space. By the end of our relationship, she couldn't work if I was in the house or if I had gone out to the office and neglected to close any one of the three doors that separated us. Space isn't always about the physical dimensions of a room.

Beth and Sandra spent a long time thinking about space and its implications before they moved in together with their seven children. "We were lovers for two years," Sandra starts their story, "before we started living together, and it took nearly that long to get comfortable with how we were going to do it. It's not like a family the size of ours can find a house just anywhere." Sandra was concerned about Megan and how it would be for her to live in a household where all of the other children were hearing. "It felt different to go from Megan—the youngest—always being protected by Jeanie and Colin, to a house where there would be more kids and less individual attention for her. One positive thing about it, though, was that all of Beth's kids knew and used sign language. They grew up with it."

And then there were the sheer logistical problems of where to put all seven children and in what arrangement. "Ed and Samuel, Beth's oldest two, were seven and eight, I think. Obviously those two would share a room, and Beth and I would share a room." She's laughing now, counting on her fingers to keep track. "And then we had five more children: my Megan, who was four, and her two youngest, Rachel and David, who were three and four, and then Colin was in the middle at six and Jeanie was eight, but she couldn't room with the boys. We had to figure out how many rooms and in which configuration."

"Actually, since we didn't rush it," Beth picks up the story, "the kids got to know one another." I tell them I can see that their becoming a couple had complexities I never dreamed of. They ended up in a row house that was narrow and had four floors with lots of small rooms. The room arrangements shifted as they settled in as a family. First the older children were on the top floor, then the younger, then Beth and Sandra, and then the family space—kitchen, living room, TV room. "That lasted about six months," says Beth, "until we realized we couldn't stand having *everyone* traipse through our part of the house on the way to theirs. Now we're on top and everyone knows they have to signal before they come up to our space."

Does everyone use sign language, I wonder? What is dinner like at their house? "Very noisy," Sandra says, grinning, "just like any other house. The TV plays loud *and* it has captions for Beth, and later, when Megan learns to read, for her too. Now one of the kids will sign a show for her. The kids who talk, talk loud *and* they all sign. And without exception, they can all holler when they want attention."

This home is Sandra and Beth's version of paradise, something they worked and planned toward for years. It wouldn't suit all of us, but the thought they put into figuring out what each of them would need guaranteed a level of satisfaction with their living situation.

Some of us may think such planning is a luxury only the upper middle class can afford, but for Barbara and Susan, planning their ideal home kept them sane in the years they were crowded into a small tract house in a development. "I didn't mind so much that our bedroom was in the basement next to the laundry," Susan remembers, "because we were committed to somehow buying a little piece of land and building our own house. Barbara wanted a shop where she could do cabinetmaking. I've always wanted a room of my own that I could decorate and use for sewing or meditating—just a small place that was mine. When I moved into Barbara's house, she was in one small bedroom upstairs and her daughter, Jeanie, was in the other. If Jeanie was home, it was hard to feel like we could make love. Then I got pregnant, and we knew we were going to need yet another space, so we started sheetrocking an area in the basement to make a room. When we moved down there, after Darien was born, we did have a little more privacy."

"Space isn't that important to us," says Mariana. "It kind of feels normal to be living on top of one another like this. And it's what we can afford right now. Why complain?" I'm curious about her acceptance. Her partner, Lisa, does her creative work—acting—largely outside of their home, but Mariana wants to write. What's that like for her, writing in a one-bedroom apartment piled high with clothes, props, old textbooks, and a large living-room couch that folds out for company and is frequently occupied? "Normal," Mariana says, laughing. "And in some ways, this is my subject, how we're living, how my people have had to live in this country and back in Honduras." She shrugs. "If I had that nice room of my own that Virginia Woolf wanted, I don't know if I could write. Of course, I'd take the yearly income she was talking about. I wouldn't have any trouble with that."

Lisa agrees that they are comfortable with their home, not that they wouldn't take a larger apartment if it became available and they could afford it. "I think Mariana ought to have a place to go and shut the door," she says slowly. Mariana is out at work now. "Part of what she writes about is how hard it is to write, and I wonder if she had her own place, if maybe she could go on to something else. I don't know." I ask Lisa about the clutter, does it bother her? "Clutter?" she looks around the living room. "It's a little crowded, is that what you mean?"

It isn't, but I let go of the question. I am always amazed at our ability to find like minds when it comes to how we live. And when I say "we" in this context, I really do mean lesbians, since there is no way to make the same comparison for a heterosexual couple. Women have picked up and cleaned up after men for so long it is almost impossible to have this conversation with a heterosexual couple. But time after time lesbians told me how easy it was to live with their lovers "in that respect anyway." And heterosexual women frequently get a longing look on their faces when they think about having a companion who shares the "housekeeping" chores without acting as though it were an enormous favor.

When lifestyles don't match, when what is crowded to one seems like clutter to another, when dirt means three weeks without vacuuming to one and two days without to another, then we have to negotiate. Beth and Sandra have different levels of being able to ignore the pile-up of dishes. "We have rotating chores for the whole family," Beth tells me. "When it's Sam and Ed's turn to do the dishes, I find myself starting to get tense. They'll put it off and put it off and finally it's 'Well, I thought you wanted us to go to bed, but if you want us to stay up and do the dishes, we will.' So I start yelling at them as soon as they push away from the table. It makes Sandra a little crazy." Sandra says she'd rather leave the dishes and not have the fuss. But it *matters* to Beth, so she takes it on.

Deborah and Peggy went through a series of adjustments when they started living together. "We're two grown women with children. We're used to doing it our way, whatever way that is. Peggy used to do the laundry once a week. She'd throw everything in at once, darks, lights, it didn't matter to her. Make me crazy," says Deb. "So now the laundry is my job, since it mattered to me. And she does the cooking more than me. I could eat anything, but Peg likes a regular meal, served sitting down at the table. That matters to her, so she does it most often."

A good place to begin negotiating is where it matters. Not just in making a match with levels of neatness or nutrition, but in figuring out how much space we need, how much money we have to spend on basics versus extras, and—one of the larger issues for lesbians, I've found—whether we share our financial resources and if so how we share them.

Money:
Hers, Hers, and Ours

When Jan and I met, she was earning about four times as much a year as I was, but I had more savings. She'd been supporting two children on her income and had little left over. Part of moving in together was merging our financial resources. It was easier than figuring who owed what or creating a percentage system based on what we were earning or might earn. It was both easy and possible for us because neither of us had any particular issue around money. In our adult lives, we were both middle class and had always been able to earn what we needed. We didn't need to measure and we didn't need to discuss what was "fair" in some abstract realm. In short, money was not one of the things that "mattered" to us in a deep, deep place.

From the first month we lived together we had one checking account with both of our names on it and two savings accounts, ditto. Neither of us kept a separate account—and we made all of these decisions about our finances before we decided to have a wedding or celebration of commitment. That ceremony marked our choices; it did not make them possible.

Most of our friends do it differently. Even those who have a joint account for living expenses keep separate accounts for other things. The list of "other" ranges from car payments to vacations to school expenses, repayment of previous loans, and just indulgences. Some say they do it for business and taxes. Others are quite clear about needing a personal financial base for emotional reasons.

"I was married for twelve years," said Sandra. "I never had my own checking account. My father wrote the checks that paid for my first year of college tuition and after that my husband wrote them. I needed to manage my own money. Whether it was child support or what I'd earned, I had to figure it out for myself." Beth had her own checking account when she was married and had no intention of giving that up when she started living with Sandra. "It wasn't an independence issue for me, exactly." She hesitates. "I think I was just used to doing it that way. Not that my husband and I shared expenses. His income paid for most of our joint expenses. But I was the one who wrote the checks, balanced the books, decided on our insurance and investments, that sort of thing." Sandra and Beth have similar incomes now, and they share the expenses for themselves and the children equally. They haven't taken a long vacation or made a major purchase in the three years they've lived together, although the station wagon Beth drives is on its last legs, and they are talking about how to finance a new family car.

Lisa and Mariana say that they have kept their incomes separate. "I never had enough money that I could trust anybody else with it," says Lisa. She hastens to add, "Not that I don't trust Mariana, it's just that it's an *issue* for me." Lisa earns more than Mariana at this point, but they still contribute equally to their household expenses. "It's an issue for me, I guess, to feel like I'm a full partner in our life here," Mariana explains. "I don't want Lisa to decide what we're going to buy to replace our old mattress just because she's going to pay more for it. She's not. I'm paying half." Mariana is stubborn about this and Lisa has been upset with her at times when they could have had something nicer or had something useful sooner if Mariana had let her pay more.

The one exception they make is their vacation fund. "I'd never go on vacation without her," Lisa insists. "What fun would that be? So we started our vacation fund. Mariana has this habit of saving her pocket change at the end of the day, and every month or so she goes to the bank and puts in whatever she's collected. I put in a certain percentage of what I get from acting gigs. Usually about twenty-five percent, unless something heavy is going on, like last year when I needed a crown for a broken tooth." They don't keep track of who puts how much in this fund, they just take a vacation when they've saved enough for a week in Florida or a weekend on Long Island. Lisa guesses she puts in about four times what Mariana does, and she's glad to do that. "We'd be in our seventies before we had a vacation, otherwise."

Ann is nearly seventy and has no intention of joining her financial life to anyone else's ever again. "I did it a couple of times, back when I was in my thirties. It never worked then and I don't see why it should now." Her voice is still edged with anger forty years later as she tells me how she and a lover bought a small ranch together. "I was a fool. I put down most of the money from what I'd saved, but we put the deed in both of our names. After a few years, she was drinking a lot and started fooling around. I told her to get out, but she said she owned half of it and I could leave or pay her to leave. I lost everything. And I was raising a daughter." Ann says romance and finances don't mix. She sees younger lesbians going down the same path she did and wants to warn them about the pitfalls. "But they don't listen. They're in love. It will be fine. She's different. Ha. I tell them, Don't come whining to me when she moves her new girlfriend into the spare bedroom."

Part of me wants to laugh at Ann's vehemence, but her heartache is real and deep. And I've seen women in my own generation suffer in the same way. One friend's lover moved her new lover and her child into the spare bedroom. I want to ask, How can these things happen in a sane world? But love, often, isn't sane.

Lesbians today are trying a variety of financial arrangements aimed at making the interface between romance and money less fraught. Couples who come from different class and educational backgrounds sometimes recognize their difference in earning power by prorating their expenses. The partner who earns more pays a higher percentage into the mutual fund. Sometimes this is based on actual earnings, sometimes on earnings and savings, sometimes on earning potential. As their incomes change, so can the assessment of what percentage each pays toward their mutual expenses.

Kathryn will be working as a physical therapist while her lover, Wanda, goes through medical school. She may see herself investing in their future together, when Wanda will be earning far more than she is and they will both be benefiting from her medical training. How does Kathryn ensure her lover's good faith?

Some couples are using legal contracts, similar to the prenuptial contracts heterosexual couples have popularized. While these contracts may or may not be legally enforceable, for many lesbians, the contract's legality is less important than seeing written down in print what the actual agreements, assumptions, and understandings are that they are operating on. Many years ago, a friend named me the legal guardian of her daughter in case anything happened to her and her lover. My friend knew that her daughter's father would have the real legal claim to her child if this happened. My claim would have no legitimacy. But she said she had named me in her will to let this child know that there was a lesbian who had been an aunt and caretaker to whom she could turn, someplace she could go on school holidays if she was in college, a home that looked something like her own if she ever needed it. Fortunately, that child is an adult today and her mother is still around for her to turn to, but she used her will to express an intention that bound us all more closely together.

Contracts that lesbians make regarding their money—like prenuptial agreements, wills, and other contracts of intent—vary from state to state with regard to the details that make them legally enforceable. But it has been my experience that putting our intentions down on paper in prose that we both can understand is never a wasted effort in human relations, particularly in couple relations.

While contracts may seem like a good way to ensure the financially negotiable parts of a relationship, it is also true that there is no such thing as "couples insurance." Nothing, absolutely nothing, *guarantees* that the woman you love today will be the woman you love tomorrow, or that the woman who has treated you fairly, thus far, will continue to do so, or that what seemed fair to you yesterday will seem equally fair tomorrow. The glue that binds long-term couples has little to do with legalities or insurances. It has much more to do with good humor, flexibility, and the ability to absorb, even enjoy, life's contradictions.

Lesbian Couples and the
World of Legalities

*I*t's the American way. We've moved in together. Maybe we rented for a year or two, the shakedown period. Now we're going to buy a house. Together.

That's what Jan and I did. We weren't really looking, but when we saw this house, we realized we could live in that space, really enjoy living in that space, and it was more affordable than our apartment. Why not?

The next morning, I called my insurance company. A simple task. We want home owner's insurance on the house we are buying. We can insure *you*, the polite woman tells me, but we can't insure your roommate with you. My insurer, alleged to be one of the best in the country, is a closed group, and my lover doesn't qualify. She doesn't qualify because we are not legally married. The woman tells me they can insure the house and all of my belongings, but not my lover's. I tell her we don't distinguish "mine" and "hers," and if we don't, how can the insurance company? There is no answer. I'll refer it to underwriters, she tells me. You do that, I respond, but I know they won't insure us together, and I slide into that familiar depression. This should have been easy. Now it's an issue. Sure, we can and have found another insurance company. But I wanted it to be easy.

This conversation is not an isolated event. Any of us who have bought a house as a couple in the so-called "domestic partnership" category know how the continual attrition of small incidents like these drains our energy. And they happened in spite of the fact that we found a gay real-estate agent who recommended a "gay-friendly" mortgage company and loan officer, escrow and title company, house appraiser, and, yes, even a termite inspector.

If we lived in New York City today—or in one or two other urban centers—we could register as domestic partners and be eligible to hold on to the rental lease if one of us died. Other than that? Domestic partnership won't guarantee that I'd be able to be insured under her medical insurance or that my insurance group will recognize her. It might get me into her hospital room if there's an emergency, but a medical power of attorney would probably be more useful. We measure our gains in social and economic terms inch by painful inch, not by yards or miles. Each inch also has its down side. It makes us more visible, and to some extent more vulnerable.

Joan and Marty remember a situation that illustrates this point exactly, a situation in which they wish their friends had thought to write a will. Several months after they bought a vacation cabin in the Adirondacks with another lesbian couple, that couple was killed in a terrible automobile crash. "We were devastated." Marty's voice still shows the loss as she speaks slowly. "Those women were our closest friends. They'd been a couple about as long as we had, we shared interests, we told one another all our secrets." But Marty and Joan didn't have to deal only with the loss of their friends. There was no will and the cabin was not joint tenancy (right of survivorship), so two families descended on Joan and Marty, horrified to learn that their daughters had been lesbians, and determined to eradicate any evidence of that fact. "We wanted to have a memorial service, bury their ashes together up at the cabin. But we didn't have a chance." Joan is bitter still at this memory. "The bodies were taken away from us and shipped out, one to the Midwest and the other to Florida, where they were buried in family plots. The families wanted the money out of the cabin instantly, and we didn't have any money, so the place we had loved, that meant so much to all four of us, was put on the market and sold at a loss. In about three months it was all over, and our lives had been irrevocably changed, and we had absolutely nothing to say about it."

Many of us have heard about the nationally publicized case of Karen Thompson and Sharon Kowalski, closeted lovers who were separated one night by a car accident that left Sharon paralyzed and speechless. Karen tried to help Sharon through rehabilitation, but Sharon's parents didn't want her to have any contact with their daughter, especially after Karen revealed to them the nature of her relationship with Sharon. Rather than making life easier, Sharon's parents took their daughter away, and it was five years, long years of legal and publicity battles, before Karen was able to see her lover again. The poignant book Karen wrote, which tells about her long struggle to be reunited with Sharon, also includes samples of some legal forms (such as different kinds of power of attorney) that might have made this a very different story if she and Sharon had been able to plan their life together without fear of their relationship's being exposed.[2]

Contracts, wills, and other legal arrangements *can* work to our benefit. When Barbara and Susan decided to go into the carpentry business together, they filed partnership registration papers with the state and county. Because they were adding Susan to Barbara's carpentry business of the same name, a friend who was a lawyer advised them to take a couple of extra steps to make sure everything in their partnership was clean and clear. "Because we were lovers," Susan says, "I didn't think we had to bother. I knew Barbara hadn't been doing anything sleazy or underhanded. Even if I hadn't been a partner then, I mean, I was on the premises. I *knew* her, you know."

What's the point of this story? "We did it anyway because the lawyer was a friend and she insisted and we didn't want to offend her, so we let her file a paper saying I wasn't liable for anything that happened in the business before the date I became a partner. Don't you know, a few months later a former client decided to sue Barbara because a sliding door on a shower stall didn't hang right. It was stupid, but if we'd both been involved, we could have been tied up for months, our income from the partnership might have been threatened." The real point of the story is that lesbians are no different from anyone else when it comes to protecting themselves from the vagaries of the legal world. Shortcuts, even when they're taken in good faith because we're lovers, we're family, we live together and share everything, can rebound and cause us enormous grief.

Jan and I are quite sure our families will recognize our relationship if something happens to one of us. We can't imagine her family or mine trying to take the house away from the survivor of our relationship, or any other animosity. In spite of this, we have wills, health-care proxies, durable powers of attorney, *and* we keep these documents current and accurate for the state in which we are living. I don't want ever to rush to the emergency room if something happens to her and be told I can't come in because I'm not a family member. It was hard enough when my father was dying to remember that the nursing staff believed Jan and I were sisters, both his daughters, a necessary fiction created so they would admit Jan to his room and speak about his condition to whichever one of us could visit. "You are both my daughters," he said. Both he and his wife concurred in this fiction.

As AIDS devastated their community, gay men learned quickly the necessity of making their ties to one another as strong and durable as possible. For several years, at the beginning of the AIDS crisis, we heard story after story of lovers rejected by their lovers' biological families, of partners kicked out of rent-controlled apartments upon the death of the person named in the lease, of HIV-positive partners being denied a lover's insurance settlement when he died, a settlement that would have meant the difference between his own impoverished death or death with dignity. We have all learned a great deal through others' tragedies, and one way of honoring the struggles of those who led the way is by not letting ourselves be similarly trapped.

Wills and other documents expressing our intentions can be simple or elaborate, and most of us hope the circumstances in which we use them will not be as drastic as those Karen Thompson faced. But not to create a will, powers of attorney, health-care proxies, or living wills, not to talk about difficult scenarios with your lover and other close friends leaves a lesbian couple vulnerable. Heterosexual marriages create automatic legal ties. Our marriages do not. We must rely on other legal vehicles to make those connections and ensure—as best we can—that our lovers and families-of-choice are not punished by legal relationships that are recognized before our own.

Sex When It's Not a Date

When I ask lesbians I know what the one thing was that changed the most when they began living together, the answer is almost invariably not about families, not about money, not about more or less space or figuring out who did what chores, nor about the world's expectations of them as a couple, it's about sex. Hundreds of different life circumstances create our desire, and they can also uncreate it. So let's face it. Living together *isn't* the same as dating, especially when it comes to sex.

"When Deborah and I first got together," remembers Peggy, "you know, *first* got together, like the first couple of months, we were at it every day, sometimes two or three times a day. It was great, but as time went on and we started to live together and I surfaced back at work and began to deal with life, you know, my desire went down a little. It went down faster than hers. I thought maybe it was my fault. I mean, she was the first and only woman I'd ever been with, so I didn't have a lot to compare it to."

So what happened, I wanted to know? Obviously it was a glitch in the relationship, not a disaster, since Deborah and Peggy have gone on for ten years since those first few months. "I want sex every day," says Deborah. "I did then and I do now. But some things are more important than others, and if Peg's preoccupied with a problem at work or something comes up with Darrell at school, well, I just have to let it go. If we went for weeks without having it, then I'd worry, but that's not what we're talking about here."

Letting it go is all well and good if that is truly what happens, but we've all known relationships in which sex or no sex was held as a bargaining chip for other concessions in the relationship; and, needless to say, those relationships don't last long. Deborah can "let it go," she says, because she and Peggy are physically close. They hug, touch, kiss, and are affectionate. "And at night," Deborah says, smiling, "we sleep like spoons. I need to feel her breasts against my back. Then I know it's okay, whatever else has happened that day. Or hasn't happened."

Life does intervene. Jobs. Children. Schedules. Emergencies. What's a dyke to do? I have friends who just celebrated their fifteenth anniversary who make Friday night "date night," no matter what else is happening. Neither of them will make other plans that night. I know never to bother to call them after 4 P.M. on Friday afternoon. I won't get them. Not at dinner, not in the evening, not later. I don't think they've missed date night more than once or twice in their whole fifteen-year history. It's a ritual, and it's more than that—a time to dress up, they tell me, to relax, to focus on one another. Without that focus, sex . . . well, it might never happen.

Barbara and Susan say sex changed for them when they began living together. "We didn't date for very long, because I had to have a place to live," Susan reiterates, reminding me that she was still living with her husband when she first was lovers with Barbara. "But when you're living together, it's hard to send the child out to a friend's every time you want to make love. And our house had very thin walls." I know a lot of couples who perfected the silent orgasm, the open-mouth, quiet heavy breathing, couples who make love on the floor so the bed springs won't make a symphony of complaint, who turn the stereo on loud even when they prefer the silence of the night. Some couples have the luxury of meeting at home during the day while the children are at school, but they are very rare. Barbara and Susan made this choice fairly frequently when they began working together. "We'd go home for lunch if we were on a job close enough. It was kind of illicit, and that made it exciting. Sometimes we'd make love instead of eating and have to gulp a sandwich in the van on the way back to the job." She laughs at the memory. "Just one of the benefits of being self-employed."

"We practically stopped having sex after we'd been living together nine months," Lisa tells me. "I've heard about lesbians who live together for ten years or so and never have sex after the first six months, but I never thought it would happen to me." Has it, I ask her? She and Mariana have been lovers for seven years, living together for five. Has it been five years without sex? "No." She laughs, teasing me. I'm trying to think what to ask next. I start with wanting to know why they stopped making love; what was that about? "Hmmm. It was just familiarity." Lisa is nodding her head, agreeing with her own assessment. "That we took one another for granted."

This is interesting. I've talked to other lovers who took one another for granted, but sex didn't stop. For some it became rote, a way to wake up or go to sleep, something they did regularly like brushing their teeth, whether they felt like it or not. This is one way, in fact, that some long-term lovers guarantee that the sex in their relationship doesn't stop. But Lisa and Mariana, they tell me, are romantics. "We want sex to be exciting, passionate," Mariana gestures. "When it stops being that, why bother?"

They learned the hard way that, for them, lovemaking has to be planned and nurtured. When it wasn't, Lisa was drawn to another woman, and the relationship nearly imploded. "Mariana wouldn't let it die, though," Lisa tells me. "She fought back. She forced me to look at what I was doing. Or about to do. In the end, I had to agree that we hadn't played out this relationship yet, so I dropped the new-potential person and we tried to put the passion back." They won't say exactly how that happened, but I gather it had to do with a weekend on Fire Island—that and a hot tub and a starry, starry night were some of the elements in recreating the passion. Keeping the passion had some of the same elements, that and good planning so that Lisa and Mariana had time in each week to focus on one another.

When I talked with Leslie and Daphne about boundaries, Leslie's sarcastic remark about "lesbian bed-death" fascinated me. Why the third month, I ask her? The twelfth month is more what I've heard, right before the first anniversary.

"I made it up," Leslie confesses. "That's about how long I expect I'd last in a monogamous relationship before I got bored." Right. So what happens to sex in a nonmonogamous relationship that goes long term? "It's not much different, probably," Leslie concedes. "I have to be careful not to think about sex with women other than Daphne as more exciting. We have friends who call themselves lovers but almost never make love with one another. Their central relationship is for support and living arrangements and things like that. I'm with Daphne because she's the most exciting woman I know. I don't want to lose track of that."

How do they keep track of it? The same as most other long-term couples. Like my friends, Leslie and Daphne have date night. It is a time for them to go out together, usually on a Saturday, often to parties with their friends, to a bar in the city, occasionally to a concert or movie. What they do isn't as important as the fact that they do it. "And we always know we'll make love when we get home," Leslie assures me. Then she grins. "And sometimes before we get home." Depending.

"I think the most important thing to remember," said Margaret softly, "is that passion waxes and wanes." She isn't talking about her new relationship with Ann, but about her twenty-five-year partnership with Rachel, who was killed in an accident seven years ago. "Intimacy, passion, sexual desire, sometimes it's there intensely and sometimes it's not. The gift of being with someone a long time is that it usually comes back. At least it did for us." How did they handle the times when it wasn't there, I wondered? "Gently." Margaret smiles at the memory. "That's not hard when both of you are off somewhere else—on some project or too busy to notice. But when it's only one of you . . . " Rachel, Margaret tells me, was a woman of mercurial enthusiasms. She never did anything by halves. Margaret, as a result, was the one who often was waiting for Rachel's energy to refocus on her, on the relationship. "But it was always worth the wait," she asserts.

"Relationships that are bound by elastic are much stronger than those that can't stretch apart and come closer. It gives the tension someplace to go."

Sexual intimacy. Not easy, not simple, whether we live together or separately. When we move past "the dating period," past that first rush of adrenaline or lust or terror that creates the initial excitement of a relationship, we are committing ourselves to maintenance—the work that shapes and builds the relationship.

We're Lovers but
We're Not Having Sex

During my first year as a single lesbian, I began seeing a woman who said she was single also. She just happened to be living with the woman who used to be her lover. They weren't lovers anymore, she insisted, because they hadn't had sex for over a year. I believed her. That they weren't lovers, I mean. Her companion, however, didn't know they weren't lovers. She knew they weren't having sex; but they slept naked in the same bed every night, and she thought they were still lovers. Until I came on the scene.

I excused myself from the relationship and considered it an aberration, a momentary glitch; maybe I hadn't been paying attention. And then it happened again. Not quite the same way. This time, when a new woman in my life said she was living with her ex, I asked to be invited to dinner and was. Everything was out in the open, and so I thought it would be fine to go ahead and get involved. It was only after I'd called her late in the evening a couple of times and she whispered into the phone and went into another room to talk that I realized she was still sleeping with her ex. Do you sleep nude, I asked her? Of course. And their relationship was far from over, whatever they were telling themselves.

I had to ask myself what was going on here. Are apartments really that hard to find in this town? Am I the only lesbian this has ever happened to? No, was the answer to both.

Sarah and Joline had a five-year period in their twenty-year relationship when they weren't having sex, weren't talking about it, and didn't know what it meant. In retrospect, they tell me this sexual hiatus grew out of insecurity: insecurity about who they were together and individually. "After a couple of years," Joline says, "I thought we had changed and were probably just like other roommates. I guess the problem came because we didn't talk about it, none of it. We didn't talk about the fact that we were making love, and when it stopped we didn't talk about that. So when this guy at the hospital kept asking me to go out with him, I couldn't see why not." She laughs a little ruefully, and I guess that Sarah showed her why not. She nods. "I told her sort of casually at dinner that I was going to an art film with a guy from work. I was nervous about saying that, which ought to have given me a clue, but Sarah didn't say anything. She just kind of shrugged. And off I went."

"When she got home," Sarah tells her part of it, "I let fly with the first plate as she came through the door. Not at her, you know, just at the wall beside the door." It was a statement, of sorts. It wasn't the only plate that was thrown that night. Sarah has since learned to articulate her needs in the relationship more clearly, but when that happened, she was twenty-five, had never lived with anyone except her parents and Joline, and had no idea that there were people who approved of lesbian relationships.

"We weren't having sex," she thinks, "because we'd become more aware of what we were doing and what people might say about us. When we first became lovers, we were girls. It was our secret and we really didn't have any models, positive or negative. Becoming aware was first a process of absorbing all of the negative stereotypes about homosexuality." The possibility of being "like" those negative stereotypes was certainly enough to quench desire, even if there had been no concurrent fear of discovery.

"I just couldn't imagine my daddy finding out," Joline admits softly, speaking of her father, the Baptist minister. "I couldn't think of what I would say to him." Can she imagine it today? "I think so. We haven't told him. Even now that he's retired from the church. But today I'm not confused about who I am and I don't think it's bad or evil. So if it came down to it, yes, I could tell him how I love Sarah."

Desire and then sex returned to Sarah and Joline's relationship once they named to themselves what they meant to one another. The end result of the plate throwing was positive, something they can laugh about today. But at the time, Sarah admits, "I never felt more evil in my life, and if talking about things can keep me from having that feeling, then I'm going to talk."

Sarah and Joline's sexual tensions were unique to their relationship, but many couples have found their sex lives affected by circumstances outside the relationship, whether it is a question of family expectations or social norms. For Joan and Marty, the lack of sexual expression wasn't caused by factors outside the relationship, but some of those external social pressures made it more difficult for them to address the problem.

"I couldn't talk to anyone," Joan remembers. "Here we were, the most out feminist couple in four counties, and for the last eight years of our fifteen-year 'perfect' relationship, we weren't having sex. Not at all. Not once. Zip."

Was it the alcohol? I asked. "Sure, that was part of it. Toward the end anyway. It made it easier in some ways. If I got horny, I'd drink to tamp it down. If I got mad at her because we weren't having sex, I'd drink to tamp it down. Or if she was mad at me. A drink answered any question I might have."

Joan suffered from a fairly common lesbian ailment: the need to keep up an image. Those of us who have come to terms with our sexuality in the comforting shade of "gay pride" have also had to come to terms—at some point—with the realization that we can't always be perfect, no matter what the movement's latest publicity report looks like. "I guess that was part of it," Joan admits. "I was seeing a straight therapist for some of that time—about the drinking—and I was protecting our relationship. But it wasn't just with straight people. I didn't want *anyone* to know that I was a lesbian who wasn't having sex with her lover. I guess I wasn't comfortable with that myself." She gave a half-laugh. "It's almost like those two things don't go together: a celibate lesbian."

One cause of the "celibate lesbian living with a lover" syndrome has been written about: female gender patterning and expectations. In brief, women are not raised with the expectation that we will initiate sex; we will respond to the overtures of men.[3] When both of the players are women, one of them has to break that expectation. When only one woman in a couple relationship is the initiator, she can feel burdened by being the one who always has to ask, to have the energy or desire, to make the first move toward being sexual.

In Wanda and Kathryn's relationship, Wanda is the initiator. Both women agree that if they waited for Kathryn to initiate sex they wouldn't have it at all. Or hardly at all. I asked Wanda how she feels about that. Her shrug says it doesn't matter, but after a moment's reflection I can see there is more to it. "It's not that I mind initiating," she says finally, "but it would be easier if she let me know sometimes when she's willing. Like flirt with me or something. We tend to get in a rut. I want to be surprised occasionally."

Being surprised occasionally seems like an excellent guideline for many parts of a couple relationship, but especially when it comes to sex. "Maybe tomorrow" or "I'm too tired tonight" or "I'll think about it after we get through this week" lets us off the hook without making us look at what is really going on in a relationship. Sex in a long-term relationship seems to work best when it is something both partners take some responsibility for—however they choose to define that.

There are, of course, celibate lesbians, women who know they are lesbians and are choosing not to be sexual. And there are celibate lesbian couples, some of them women who have lived together for many years without ever expressing their affection for one another sexually, others who have let that part of their relationship diminish without regret. The reasons for their choices are various and no less valid than they are for those of us who are choosing to be sexual. Because sex *is* a choice.

When we think there is only one way to "be" lesbians, when we let others' definitions of who we are or what we do limit us, when we pay more attention to "what they think" than to our own desires, we are giving away our choices. We also give away our choices if we accept dysfunction as a normal part of a relationship. The key to whether we are choosing a path or being forced down it usually has to do with our comfort level. When the path is freely chosen, we don't have to drink to make it palatable, we don't have to stuff our anger to make the road smoother, we don't have to hide what we are "really" doing from our friends, we don't feel ashamed to be found out.

REFERENCES

1. Judith McDaniel, "November Passage,"*November Woman*, Glens Falls, New York: Loft Press, 1983, p. 9.

2. Karen Thompson and Julie Andrzejewski, *Why Can't Sharon Kowalski Come Home?* San Francisco: Spinster/Aunt Lute, 1988.

3. D. Merilee Clunis and G. Dorsey Green, *Lesbian Couples.* Seattle, Washington: Seal Press, 2nd ed., 1993, pp. 71–76.

RESOURCES

Organizations that help with legal information:

The National Center for Lesbian Rights
870 Market Street, Suite 570
San Francisco, CA 94102
415-392-6257

The center also publishes the following information pamphlets:
Preserving and Protecting the Families of Lesbians and Gay Men (1990).
Recognizing Lesbian and Gay Families: Strategies for Obtaining Domestic Partner Benefits (1992).

The American Civil Liberties Union
The Lesbian and Gay Rights Project
132 West 43rd Street
New York, NY 10036
212-944-9800

With affiliates in every state, the ACLU is the nation's oldest civil liberties organization. The Lesbian and Gay Rights Project was founded in 1986; it initiates its own legal projects and acts as network and information center for each affiliate.

The ACLU also publishes the following information:

The Rights of Lesbians and Gay Men: The Basic ACLU Guide to a Gay Person's Rights. Southern Illinois University Press, 3rd ed., 1992.

For a practical understanding and philosophical/political discussion of the laws affecting lesbians, see Ruthann Robson, *Lesbian (Out)law: Survival Under the Rule of Law* (Ithaca, NY: Firebrand Books, 1992). Robson asks how lesbians can use the law without being used by it.

PART SIX

Parenting

Lesbian Mothers?

*I*n the late 1970s I made several annual appearances before a class of second-year medical students at the local medical college to talk about lesbian sexuality and lesbian health concerns to the men and women who were going to become our doctors. A gay man spoke on the same occasions, usually preceding me. The first time we did the event together, I was rather awed at the variety of diseases he presented as particular to gay men: venereal diseases, of course, but also hepatitis and hemorrhoids were common, frequent problems.

When it was my turn to speak, I mentioned the disease of addiction, which strikes the lesbian and gay community more frequently than the average. I enjoyed being able to cite statistics that showed venereal diseases in the lesbian community were almost nonexistent. And I said lesbians are women and we have all of the medical problems that women have. "But you don't have children," one of the medical students challenged me. "Wrong," I told him. "Many lesbians have had children, usually in a heterosexual marriage. Don't assume a woman with children is not a lesbian, and don't assume a lesbian won't have children."

That was in 1976 or 1977. I didn't know any lesbian who had conceived a child through artificial insemination, nor had any lesbian couples I knew tried to become foster parents or adopt a child. We thought about it, we talked about it, but none of us had tried it yet.

But my *impression* of lesbians, even from a rather limited circle of acquaintance, was that many of us had children and that we were living quiet and unobserved lives in every corner of the country.

When a partner and I were considering adopting a child nearly fifteen years ago, a closeted lesbian social worker told us it would be possible if . . . If only one of us was named in the adoption, if we concealed our relationship, if we were willing to take a "difficult to place" child.

The first woman I knew who decided to have a child by artificial insemination, in 1984, was also aware of potential legal difficulties. To forestall a paternity claim by a biological father, she had a friend who was a nurse interview three potential donor fathers, none of whom knew who the mother would be. The nurse then collected semen from two of the willing donors, and the mother was inseminated. Paternity *could* be legally proven by genetic testing, of course, but this procedure, she thought, would minimize the possibility of the biological father's even trying to find her. And this safety was important to her because her partner had just had to fight in court for the custody of her two children.

I also considered being inseminated, as did my lover at that time. I did not pursue pregnancy. I enjoyed children, I knew I could parent, but I wasn't driven to parent. I never felt my personal satisfaction or identity relied on bearing a child. Some of my friends felt different, and for them I am glad the tide of opinion and technology has made it possible for them to have children.

Today, social realities have changed. Our lives are observed. Articles are published about our families in the *New York Times* and *Newsweek*. Between 1985 and 1993, twelve books have been published for lesbian and gay parents. I know many children who were conceived through artificial insemination. I have friends who have adopted, others who are foster parents. In some cases they have faced the state social services system together as an out lesbian couple and still been successful. In other instances, one of the two has been named the parent of record, with the tacit cooperation of a social services system that chooses not to see the obvious.

For me, there were always enough children who needed attention, who needed to be singled out as special, and enough moms who needed a weekend off from parenting, so that I could discover what a fine "aunt" I made. Being an aunt is not an inconsequential task; it does not even require a biological sister or nieces and nephews. I've made an "aunt" commitment to the children of friends; and it is a commitment. When I began to develop a special relationship with a child for the first time, I very quickly realized that I had an obligation to her, no matter what happened to my friendship with her mother, no matter where else I might decide to live. If I was creating an expectation in this child that I would be there for her, I had better, in fact, be there. As a result, I've only done it twice—become an honorary aunt—because it is demanding. But the rewards? I've been allowed to watch a child grow and become an adult—not from the outside, but as a confidante and friend and mentor.

More recently, since Jan and I have been partners, I have found myself in the position of "second mom" to her children—a young woman in her mid-twenties, who does not live with us, and a young man of twenty-one, who has lived with us occasionally. I am cautious in making assumptions about what my relationship with Erica and Adam should be or will be. My father remarried when I was an adult, and it took years for me to become comfortable in my relationship with his wife, so I know how hard it can be for children to relate to a parent's new partner. I do make one assumption, however, and that is that we *are* family and will be relating to one another in that context. As partners, Jan and I have chosen to join our financial life. When one of Jan's children needed tuition for school, for example, then it became our mutual obligation to decide what we could do and when we could do it. Her children are not solely her responsibility. We are family.

And there are rewards for me, not only responsibilities. On Mother's Day this year I received my first Mother's Day card. Not a card, actually, because Adam couldn't find a card for two moms. But the letter he wrote in his own words, saying thanks for our support, was far better than any card I could have imagined.

Families of Circumstance

Most lesbians who have children today had them in the context of heterosexual marriages, often before they recognized their own lesbian sexuality. Coming out with children. It isn't the same as coming out when there's only yourself to think about. And it is different from being a heterosexual, divorced mom who falls in love with a man. Heterosexual single mothers may have a hard time, but they aren't outlaws in the same way lesbians are outlaws, and their children aren't subjected to the secrecy of a closeted household or to the teasing and ridicule of an openly lesbian household.[1]

"Having a child was always an issue for me," says Ann, who is now in her late sixties. "In my generation, it wasn't done. There weren't so many single mothers around, and you can bet not many of those considered themselves lesbians." Ann was married for three months in 1952; she was pregnant when she left the marriage and knew that—but she also knew she couldn't stay. "I knew I was a lesbian before I got married, but I couldn't live the way I saw lesbians living. I had a girlfriend when I was in high school in South Boston, and we used to go to a little dark bar in Back Bay. It was on a side street. You couldn't tell if the bartender was a man or a woman. You know the scene. She'd wear a T-shirt with the sleeves rolled up over her biceps and a pack of Camels tucked in her sleeve. I guess the older women were taking care of Kelly and me, but they told us stories that made me think I could never live like that." She pauses, reflective, searching for words to explain the "like that." "There was no joy in that life. None that I could see anyway. Being a gay girl was a burden back then. Tension. That bar was always filled with tension—who was seeing who, who belonged to . . . you know?" I nod. I do know.

"So I dumped Kelly and that whole scene. I fled. I went west, as far away from my family as I could get—St. Louis." She laughs when I look surprised. Not California? "There was a job advertised in St. Louis at a hospital. The notice was on a bulletin board at the hospital where I'd been working as an aide all during high school, and I thought I'd just go out there and apply for it. My family was wild, but I did it. By the time I got there, of course, that job was long gone; but I got another one. And put myself through training as a physical therapist. That was a new profession then. The guy I married worked at the hospital." She shook her head in wonder. "We barely knew each other. I can't think why I thought it would work, but I was having all these feelings about some of the other girls I was training with. And then I was pregnant and on my own again."

How did Ann find a woman lover? She started going to the bars again, first in St. Louis and then in San Diego, where she eventually relocated. "I didn't tell them about my daughter at first," she admits. "I got dumped too many times." Eventually she began living with a woman. They called each other roommates, and Ann was totally responsible for her child. "Emily didn't like how much time I had to spend with Sally. Sally was only three or four at the time and there wasn't a whole lot I could do about her." Emily left and Ann was single for a long time until she met Nancy, and they bought a small ranch together on the outskirts of San Diego. "We were pretty much a family," she remembers. "It was then I told Sally about me and Nancy. When she was thirteen or so. But we never told anyone else. We were just two women and a girl on a ranch with four horses and six dogs." It sounds great to me and I tell her so. "For a while," she nods, "until Nancy's drinking got real bad."

Ann says her daughter seemed to accept her mother's lesbianism, but years later told her how awful it was having to live with a secret like that, seldom bringing her friends to the house, especially in the years when she was in high school and Nancy's drinking made her unpredictable. "It's hard to know how to balance it," Ann says today. "I look back and think, Well, maybe I never should have had a lover. Maybe I owed that to Sally. But I owed myself a life too. And I did the best I could. I never wanted to hurt her. If I was living alone, I was unhappy. Would that have been better for her? I don't know."

"Yes, that still happens," Barbara told me when I asked if it was hard for lesbians with children to find lovers who were willing to take the whole package. "I had my daughter in 1973, and when I came out in '75, there were lesbians in my community who wouldn't have any-thing to do with me." As a lover, I ask, or as a friend? "Both," she answers firmly. "Not just that they didn't want to deal with a kid, but if I had a kid, it meant I'd been with a man. There was a lot of preju-dice against that."

I find that hard to understand in 1975, but Barbara lived in a rural community far away from the urban centers, where feminism was being debated and lesbians were becoming more visible. Barbara didn't know many lesbians, so being shunned hurt her, at first. "I learned pretty quickly, though, that if a woman couldn't deal with my daughter she couldn't deal with me. What was I going to do? Pretend I didn't have a child? Farm her out for adoption?" She shakes her head as though it were still hard for her to believe. "One woman told me just that. That if I got rid of the kid, she'd like to date me. I told her I couldn't just take her back to the pound like a stray dog." When Barbara met Susan, she was wary, on guard. "My daughter had a right to expect certain things of me. I wasn't going to get involved with someone who couldn't include my daughter when she was thinking about a life with me."

I was surprised at Ann's and Barbara's experiences, surprised and dismayed. Over the years I've known a lot of lesbians with children. They are part of our community, and yet . . . I've heard the debates about whether male children are welcome in women-only space, and if they are, how old they can be before they are no longer our children, but young men, part of the male community. I've heard mothers at conferences ask why child care during the workshops wasn't part of the planning. I've heard lesbians without children criticize lesbian mothers—from a safe and uninvolved distance—for not doing enough for their children and for expecting too much help from women who "just happen to be in the community."

Barbara's partner, Susan, thinks she understands part of the lesbian community's discomfort with our own children. "We're breaking away from the stereotypes when we say we're lesbians. Maybe that breaking away is about the connection between women and raising children too? You know, women as caretakers and all that."

"I don't know about that," says Peggy. "I dated men who didn't want me to have my son either. The only woman I ever dated was Deborah, and she had kids of her own." Deborah raises an eyebrow at Peg as though she's surprised they've never had this conversation. "You were such a relief," she tells Peg. "You knew what I was talking about when I said I couldn't do something because I hadn't had time to make arrangements for the kids. I know," she turns to me and waves her hand in dismissal, "black families are supposed to have this extended network of relatives that you drop the kids off with any time of day or night. But some white man with no kids made that one up. It was a relief to be with someone who could share that with me. I tell you, at one point I might have been willing to go back to men if there'd been one who was actually taking care of his kids by himself." That seems a little extreme to all three of us, and Deborah and Peggy start to laugh. It breaks the tension, but it is obvious to me how much stress Deborah experienced being a lesbian alone with two children.

What about the other side? You meet a wonderful woman; you go out a few times; you spend a couple of nights together. She's mentioned her two children. She's proud of them. You nod, smile at the right moments. And then you're in love. You want to be part of her life, want her to be in your life. What happens next? If she weren't a mother, the answer to that would be fairly straightforward. If you wanted to keep your own places, you would arrange to spend more time together, especially time that included sleepovers. Or you could move into her place, she could move into yours, or you'd look for something new together. Your desires and her desires, that's all you'd have to think about. But when you fall in love with a woman who has children, there are other people to think about. Her children. What are their rights? Her rights? Yours?

"No," says Leslie, a little nervous at her own forthrightness, "I'd never get involved with a woman who had a kid. It's not my thing, I don't want the responsibility, I don't want to have to think about it." I'm a little surprised at the vehemence of her response. Why would it be your responsibility, I want to know, especially in the earliest stages of the relationship? "Not that the child would be my responsibility," Leslie corrects, "but if I know I don't want to live with a child or even relate to one, then I have a responsibility not to get involved. And I *don't* want the responsibility of a child down the road."

Leslie's experience as a child of divorced parents colors her thinking on this subject, she readily admits. Her mother dated several men who would have preferred that Leslie and her sisters didn't exist. "Weekends with one of them were torture for all of us. It was our house, but we felt like we didn't belong there. It solved itself when my oldest sister could take care of us, and then Mother would go off to his place. We may have felt abandoned or left out, but we all knew it was better than the other way around."

Does it work that way with women, I wonder, or are we more able to include children in our lives? "More propaganda," insists Leslie. And I'm inclined to agree with her. Personal need, not gender, determines whether we want to live with children or not. For some of us, loving a woman who has children lives out our sense of family. I've known women who moved into relationships with a woman and child or children and felt that immediate sense of home, of filling in a space they hadn't known was empty. Other women have come to accept the children they have found in their lives with a much greater effort. Loving the woman, they have had to learn to love the children. Others have not come to that acceptance, and the relationship has ended.

"Children have rights. Adults have rights and responsibilities. It's that simple, believe me," says Marty, and I wonder if that's the ex-nun speaking. "Part of it's from being a teacher. You see the way children are treated. They didn't ask to be born. Sure, some of them are tough to love, especially when you're coming into the family scene from the outside." I ask her what her experience has been, in the year since she and Joan separated. Has she dated any lesbians with children?

"One, yes, sort of . . . " I see her hesitance and ask her about it. "Oh, it's not much." She tries to brush it away. "It's just a little embarrassing to admit I was jealous of a six-year-old. He was jealous of me, too, and made sure he got his mom's attention the only way he knew—either by acting out or having accidents. I'd been dating her for three months and he'd had two knock-down tantrums that were nearly seizures, and he broke his arm. I mean, how could I compete with that?" Marty was conscious of the potential for this kind of dynamic before she began dating a woman with a child. She knew what was happening while it was happening, "and still I couldn't make it be different. I don't know what you do in a situation like that. So I withdrew." She shrugs.

It is hard, and it isn't always like that, and yet I'm not quite sure what makes the difference. Susan says she doesn't remember Barbara's daughter's ever being jealous of her—at least she didn't let Barbara know it if she was. "But it was a little different for me," she says. "I went into the relationship knowing I wanted to have a child of my own and this was the family I was going to raise my child in. So I intended to be a part of Jeanie's life. I let her know that from the start."

Most of us aren't that clear about our long-term goals when we begin a relationship. Some lesbian mothers told me they wait a while before they let a new "interest" even meet their children. Others use it as a kind of test, to see which way the relationship might go. "It's not that I give my kids power over who I see and don't see," one lesbian mom explained, "but it is important to me to get their take on her. Kids are real perceptive. They know if someone's genuine or not. I don't always get involved with people they like, but if my son sort of shrugs and says, 'Eh, I guess she's okay, Mom,' then that's like getting a rave review!"

I imagine jealousy also happens in situations where both women have children. "You can count on that," Sandra says, laughing. "We not only had to deal with Beth's kids' being jealous of me and my kids and vice versa, but I was jealous of her relationship with her husband." But she left her husband to be with you, I protest. Why be jealous of him? "It's complicated," she explains. "He was being decent about the whole thing and helping Beth with the kids. She'd see him every weekend when they'd exchange the kids. I was jealous that he was helping out and my ex wasn't; and I was jealous of the time she took from me to help the kids get to their father's house and back. He only lived an hour away from us, but it always seemed like she had to go pick the kids up or something when I wanted her to be involved in what I was doing."

Other women have told me similar stories. Dealing with the complexities and intricacies of contemporary family life can be difficult, confusing, and—when it works—incredibly rewarding. "It's always a choice," Beth insists, "whether a problem is going to be an opportunity or a limitation. When it involves children, I think we have to be creative; otherwise we begin to feel like we're giving up our lives for our kids. I want my kids and I want my own life. Now. Not when they're grown up and have left home. What's most important to me about my relationship with Sandra is that we both feel this way and we both have a commitment to making it work."

Lesbians Who Become Moms

Not only are lesbian families becoming more visible; in fact, there's a lesbian baby boom. In the ten years since the first of my friends conceived a child by artificial insemination, and we all laughed about the methods of collection—"mayonnaise jars"—and the "turkey baster baby," literally thousands of lesbians have found ways to conceive children without benefit of male consorts. Back in the beginning, the reason a lesbian used her own devices to become impregnated was that her gynecologist couldn't artificially inseminate an unmarried woman. Today that has changed. And today the methods used, the relationships with donors, are as various as the women who have imagined them.

In 1984 my friend didn't want the donors to even know who she was; she sent another friend to ask them if they were interested, take their medical records, and collect the semen. Another lesbian I know, whose son is five, has a relationship with the father, a gay man; but he lives on the other side of the country and comes to see his son only once a year or so. That's plenty of contact for her. Other women have close ties to the men—gay or straight—who father their children. A national magazine featured a family with four parents and a child, a lesbian couple who conceived their child with a gay male couple by using artificial insemination, and the whole family lived together under one roof.

What are the issues today facing lesbians who want to bear children? If social mores have creaked open far enough to allow for single mothers, are there any problems?

The women I talked with said that the relationship with the sperm donor still caused a lot of discussion. For a few years, gay men seemed the way to go, but that was before HIV. Today, gay men who want to become donors need also to be willing to be tested for HIV— not once, but possibly several times, depending upon their life circumstances. In fact, a lesbian who is looking for a donor will want him to be tested no matter what his sexual preference *and* have confidence that he will practice safe sex during the period of insemination. The risks are too high; a woman can become infected with HIV through sperm that is artificially inseminated just as quickly as by having intercourse with a man. And an HIV-infected mother can give the virus to her child.

Beyond that obvious detail, however, lies an ocean of possibility and confusion. Gay man? Straight man? Married/coupled/single man? Every lesbian who has conceived a child by artificial insemination has a different story to tell and different reasons for her choices. Ten years ago, the assumption about gay men that my friend operated on was that they would not want to raise these children, but in a spirit of camaraderie would donate their seed to a lesbian who wanted to be a mom. And she found two men for whom that was true. They wanted protection, too, assurances they would not be named in a paternity suit if the financial burden became too much for a single mother.

Other women have told me about heartrending discussions and decisions involving a man who wanted to be included in a child's life when the mother-to-be only wanted to raise the child with her partner. Or a lesbian who was single and couldn't find a man who wanted to share some responsibility for a child. Or a lesbian couple who couldn't agree on a donor. Some stories have been about the successes—a woman's cousin or brother donating sperm to her lover, a lesbian who had given up trying to find the right donor meeting an old "buddy" at a high school reunion who wanted to participate, and many more.

In considering an anonymous donor, a woman needs to decide whether or not her child will have access to the father's medical records. Susan sent a registered nurse to interview potential donors. She wanted a complete medical history of both of the men who decided to donate. I wondered what good that would do her child if she didn't know which of the medical records was relevant to her. "We know," she told me, smiling. "Now we know which one it is, and I'll keep that information so that it will be available to my child if it's ever necessary."

When a child is small, the questions about a male parent are fairly simple. But when a child is old enough to ask about its father, lesbian mothers who have chosen anonymous donors need to be able to answer their questions.

The caution for lesbians who decide to conceive through artificial insemination is that we are charting new territories, both emotionally and legally, and there is very little protection out there for us. If questions of surrogate mothers, artificial insemination, and adoption are difficult for married heterosexual women, we can only expect they will be hair-raisingly difficult for lesbians. Many of the legal questions are being addressed by the books, groups, and organizations listed in the Resource section of this chapter, but the emotional issues are less easily categorized.

Two friends who conceived a child two years ago with the help of a known donor say their relationship with him is not the problem, it's with the rest of their lives. Because one of the women was obviously the biological mother (she's still nursing), the world sees her as the real mom and her partner as "the other parent." "It's not just that some of our friends don't get it, but in day care or at the doctor's office I get written down as lots of things," she tells me. "Sometimes I'm the father, sometimes the other parent, but never the mother. We're both mothers and I get angry and frustrated at having to say that all the time." And this child hasn't even gone to school yet, when the paperwork will get really interesting.

Two friends who adopted an infant have a slightly different problem. One of them works full time and the other has been able to work half time, on two long day shifts. That means she is at home with the baby more often, and friends of these women have noticed that the baby wants one of his moms more often than he wants the other. "Complete equality just isn't realistic," insists an older friend of the family, who raised three children. "There's going to be a dominant parent. That's nature's way. In the end, at any crucial moment, someone has to be in charge. You can't be checking with one another, making sure she agrees, the child agrees, you just have to act."

Their child isn't in school yet, either, but they are both the legal adopted parents. As a result, this lesbian couple will not have difficulty with school officials, who will know they can call either parent in case of an emergency. My friends who had their own child can hope that will be true—and generally schools have been willing to list both moms of children of lesbians as their parents—but there are no legal guarantees of that.

When Susan left her husband to begin the relationship with Barbara, one of the cornerstones of that relationship was her desire to have a child. It was a decision she made before she got involved with Barbara. Barbara, when asked, was absolutely against having another child in her family. Having to raise a daughter by herself, as a working-class lesbian who had access to very limited resources, was not easy for Barbara. When she met Susan, her daughter was nine, going to school, able to stay over at a friend's house occasionally. Barbara was just beginning to enjoy the freedom of having a child who was not totally dependent. "I think if we had been involved and then I made the decision to have a child," says Susan, "it probably would have been different—it probably would have split us up. But because she knew from the beginning, even before we got involved, that this was something I was going to do, she knew she'd have to accept it. I mean, when I moved in, I already had the crib."

One way Barbara was able to come to terms with Susan's decision was to let Susan know the child would be entirely her responsibility. "I don't want to coparent," she said, "and I meant it." When the baby came, in the second year of their relationship, his arrival marked a major shift for them. "I just had less time," Susan remembers, "and it was hard. I was usually exhausted because I worked and had a baby and a lover. The thing that saved me was that Barbara really did know what I was going through. She'd been there. And she was supportive. She just wasn't going to take over for me."

When Darien was about two, Barbara began to get more involved with him. She and her daughter, Jeanie, would pick him up at day care when Susan had to work late, give him his supper and a bath, so Susan could come home and put him to bed. "What I realized after a while," Barbara admits, "was that my biggest fear had been that I would be left at home again with the kids. It happened with my husband, then with a couple of lovers, who would just go off and do things without me rather than help me deal with child care. I had this image of Susan going off to a concert or to a NOW meeting and assuming I'd take care of the baby, since I had to be home with my own kid anyway." That wasn't happening, but something else was. "If I didn't help Susan out at all, she wouldn't have any time for me. Her whole energy would go to holding things together. We had no sex life the first two years of Darien's life. I got involved out of self-interest."

Susan's perspective was slightly different. "Barbara did help more," she agrees, "and I was really grateful for that, but I learned not to *ask* for help. That would set off her 'I'm being taken advantage of' response, so I had to wait and see what she wanted to do and when." How did the relationship survive its various tensions? "I was working out how to parent, since my own experience of being parented was pretty awful." Susan is smiling now, and it is obvious to me that the tension of child rearing is pretty much in the past tense. "I *needed* to be left on my own to raise Darien the way I wanted to raise him. What I did by getting involved with Barbara—although it wasn't conscious at the time—was to ensure that I couldn't slide out of that responsibility. And Barbara needed to learn to trust that I wasn't going to take advantage of her and then abandon her. It's worked well for us, actually." It has, I can see that. Barbara's daughter, Jeanie, is in college, and Darien is a self-sufficient ten-year-old, who is pleased that he has two moms when some kids only get to have one.

I ask Barbara and Susan if having children made it more important for them to work through the difficulties in their early relationship. So many women, it seems, hit those first couple of difficult times and let go of the relationship. Susan and Barbara had some large differences to resolve, and they succeeded. Why?

"I got involved with Susan in spite of the fact that she wanted this baby because she was the best thing that had ever come into my life," Barbara says with a shrug. "So she wanted this baby. I didn't see dozens of other women vying for my attention who had as much in common with me as Susan had. And I was right. I never met anybody who would have suited me better. But then I never expected to."

"I don't quite know how to say this," Susan begins hesitantly, "but one of the reasons we may have just buckled down and solved our own problems was that we weren't getting much support from the community." Which community? I asked. "The lesbian community. I had just come out by getting involved with Barbara, and one of the most wonderful things for me was finding this community of lesbians who loved what I loved—the music festivals, the dancing, our lesbian c.r. group. I was totally into it. And when I talked about having a baby, my c.r. group cheered me on." She pauses, frowning. "But when Darien was born, all that support disappeared. Him being a boy didn't help, but I don't think that was really what it was about. No one—no lesbians—offered any kind of help. I found my community changing. The women who became my friends were other mothers, straight women with kids about my son's age."

Susan's experience wasn't unique, I discovered. What is changing is not the support that lesbians without children give to their friends who have children, but that more lesbians have children and are making community with one another. This happens most commonly in areas where lesbians have begun to create a significant presence—in towns like Northampton and Provincetown, Massachusetts; Ithaca, New York; and in larger cities across the country.

"I'm a different person today than if I hadn't decided to have a child," Susan says. "I'm stronger. I've made a family for myself and I have more people to love. When I was pregnant I had this real sense of family that I never had before. I felt a sense of security. I have deeper roots. My son has given me that."

Lisa and Mariana are thinking about having a child in the future. "Somewhere between thirty and thirty-five would be good, I think," ventures Lisa. They've considered several options—each bearing a child, one having a baby, adoption. What are the issues for you? I want to know. How will you decide? We talk for quite a while and I hear some of their stories. They've joked about what race the baby will be—"Lisa could get a Latino sperm donor or I could get a black donor or we could expand and look for a gay Asian man and have kids that are . . . "—but under the levity, this is a serious issue because it involves race and culture. The real issue is that neither Lisa nor Mariana is out to her family, and both believe they would want to raise a child in the context of family, their own biological and cultural families being the center of that desire.

"Our white lesbian friends who are having children, or thinking about having children, aren't really dealing with the same things we are," Lisa tells me. "Yes, I know it's a big deal whether you can get the schoolteachers to acknowledge that you're both the mommies. I know we have to get all the forms changed that say 'mother' and 'father,' but for us that doesn't come first."

"If I have a child," Mariana begins reflectively, "I want him or her to know my grandmother. To listen to her talk about Honduras. To learn Spanish because it's spoken at home, around the dinner table, with lots of cousins and aunts and uncles. I don't see a way for that to happen right now." Nor does Lisa. Lisa's feelings of community are tied to her parents, but she senses more connection to her local African American community than Mariana seems to find in the Latino community in their city. "Face it," she says, "I'm never moving back down to Texas. Never. I do have close friends here. Theater people are a lot like family, and I have gay and straight friends with children. I guess it's just a kind of, I don't know, what's the word? Nostalgia? I'd love to see my daughter or son at a family dinner with three or four generations of relatives all there. It probably won't happen, not that way. But I do think about what would be there in place of that community."

Many lesbians who want to parent are thinking about these issues and trying to find ways to create strong family ties for their children, strong ties to their race, culture, or history. For some, this has meant inventing rituals to replace the ones they've lost or the ones that were never there. An African American friend whose son was turning thirteen wanted something comparable to a bar mitzvah for him. She wanted him to think consciously about becoming an adult and what kind of responsibilities that implied, what kind of ethics and community values he would take with him into adulthood. She invited his father, who was white, her parents and grandparents, her lover—a black woman who had parented her son with her for five years—and her college-age daughter. I spoke to her just before the event, when she was moaning, "What ever possessed me to do something like this?" and trying to juggle seating arrangements. But afterward she was exhilarated. "It's not every coming-of-age young black man who knows directly how many people helped him get this far and will be there for him in the future."

Some lesbian mothers are finding traditional religious holidays don't provide what they want for their families and are doing it differently. One child I know doesn't believe in Santa Claus. The Solstice Fairy came to her house in December and left gifts. Another friend, with a ten-year-old daughter, is doing research on Native American rituals for female coming of age, the celebration of menstruation. She wants to be ready when the time comes.

The particulars often aren't as important as the intention and the effort. Like the rituals that help create and define us as couples, family rituals are a way of marking a path for ourselves, of telling ourselves, one another, and outsiders what is most important to us.

So What About the Kids?

The headline summed up the article succinctly: "Under nearly every gay-rights issue lurks a question: What about the kids?" Not *our* kids. The concern the article refers to is that of heterosexual parents for *our* effect on *their* kids. "It cuts right to the bone," says Lon Mabon, one of the initiators of the 1992 Oregon anti-gay initiative, which was narrowly defeated. Parents, he insists, are asking themselves, "Do I want my children influenced toward homosexuality?"[2] Every gay-rights issue can be carried back to the question about the children, and this has been one of the tactics used against us. Gays in the military? Opponents ask about the Boy Scouts. Civil rights? We hear that day-care centers will be required to hire homosexual pedophiles.

When I chose not to be open about my sexuality while I was working with the Girl Scouts in a rural community, I was recognizing—and perhaps reinforcing—this prejudice. The lesbian schoolteachers in that community who created fictitious "fiancés" or boyfriends were coping in the same way. And the lesbians with children who hid their sexual orientation from their community, often from their own children, were experiencing the same pressure.

Rational people, people with some experience of the world, know that no child is "influenced toward homosexuality," any more than those of us who are lesbian and gay were influenced toward heterosexuality by our (usually, almost inevitably) heterosexual parents. It is true that most of us felt no permission—let alone encouragement—to be homosexual, which meant that we were not encouraged to be who we *were*, but to be heterosexual whatever we were. What gay-rights activists ask for all children is that they be encouraged to be themselves, to experience their own sexuality and act on it joyfully. But that is not an easy vision to convey in a homophobic world. "I don't think there's a parent alive who wants their child to be gay," says Arthur Kropp, director of the liberal constitutional watchdog group People for the American Way. "Why would you want your child to be somebody that so many people hate, because of nothing more than sexual orientation?"[3] That is a perspective we hope to change—for our own survival and for the sake of any child growing up lesbian or gay.

Just as most of us who are lesbian and gay were raised by heterosexual parents who never dreamed we might turn out "this way," so will our children choose their lovers and partners without regard for what their lesbian moms might wish for them. Years ago, when her children were small, a friend was asked to speak about being a lesbian mother to a national YWCA function in her city. After a moving talk and an interesting question-and-answer period, one of the women asked my friend, the mother of a son and a daughter, "What do you want for your children? If you could choose, wouldn't you want them to be straight?" My friend thought a moment (and told me later she'd considered lying) and admitted, "Because of what I know about women and their ability to love, I would like for my son to be loved by a woman," she paused for emphasis, "and for my daughter to be loved by a woman." What did they say, I wanted to know; were they shocked? "Shocked into some kind of recognition, I'd guess," she said. "I'm sure I saw some nods of agreement." But, in fact, whatever we wish for our children, we can't choose it for them, and today both of my friend's children are grown-up—and they're heterosexual.

What about these children we are most likely to influence? These children who grow up in our homes? A recent survey of studies about children raised by lesbian and gay parents concludes that children raised in our homes are no more likely to have problems than children raised by heterosexual parents. In a survey of the studies done in the last ten years, "what evidence there is suggests there are no particular developmental or emotional deficits for children raised by gay or lesbian parents," maintains Dr. Michael E. Lamb, chief of the section on social and emotional development at the National Institute of Child Health and Human Development. In another study, Dr. Julie Gottman, a clinical psychologist in Seattle, found that children whose mothers (whether lesbian or heterosexual) had partners living in the home tended to do "somewhat better than the others in self-confidence, self-acceptance and independence. But the sexual orientation of the lesbian mothers had no adverse effects."[4]

The so-called lesbian baby boom is fairly recent, so it will be several years before extensive studies can be done about how being raised as the child of a lesbian or gay couple affects a young person. But all of the evidence so far suggests that love and attention are far more important to children than the sexual orientation of their parents or than the homophobia they must confront as they go out into the world.[5]

In spite of this knowledge, a judge in Virginia recently removed a child from his mother's home because she was living with her lesbian lover. Sharon Bottoms lost custody of her two-year-old son, Tyler, when her mother argued that her daughter's lesbian relationship not only was illegal under Virginia's sodomy laws but was damaging to the child, that he would be "emotionally confused for life" by having two mothers. Her claim was correct as far as the seldom-enforced Virginia sodomy law was concerned, but patently incorrect about the effect of a parent's sexual orientation on the child's emotional stability. In spite of this, Judge Parsons chose to follow a 1985 Virginia Supreme Court decision that held that homosexuality was a legitimate reason for losing custody of a child.[6]

In other legal precedents, lesbians have been granted custody of their own children even when a heterosexual biological father has tried to gain that custody, and lesbian and gay couples have been allowed to adopt children together.[7] Laws vary from state to state, and the standards are still being set, but in many areas of the country lesbians are more able to defend themselves in these situations than they were even ten years ago.

One way we are conveying our vision "about the kids" to the rest of the world is by being open to and with our own children. "We are the people in your neighborhood," proclaims a flier for a Lesbian, Gay and Bisexual Parent Support Group. "Your next-door neighbor, that nice father down the street, the mom in your carpool, your child's best friend's father or mother at the PTA meeting, we are lesbian mothers and gay fathers." Lesbian and gay families with children are forming networks, having potlucks and picnics, going to gay-pride events together, planning Saturdays in the park and a wide variety of other family outings. "Any time there is a family-type event," says the organizer of one such community group, "we decide first if we want to go and then how open we want to be about who we are. The Unitarians always put us on the Family Day program, but other groups might not be so thrilled to have us. We make a judgment call. It's about creating a fun time for families, and the political impact has to be secondary."

The hardest time for children of lesbians—as reported in the studies available and as reported by my many friends and acquaintances who have "been there"—is adolescence. Children may start to notice differences in their families as early as first or second grade, but it is in junior high school that the pressure from peers gets really intense. Jan remembers a couple of early teen years when Adam hid certain books and papers when he would bring a friend home from school. And then she noticed he wasn't doing that anymore. "How come?" she asked him. He shrugged. "I got tired of it. I just told them all you're a lesbian." After she got over her shock at having been "outed" in the local school scene, she was pleased and relieved. The parents of one of his friends had trouble dealing with their daughter's visiting in the home of a lesbian mother, but it was never an issue for Adam or Jan after that.

Children of gay parents have formed their own networks. Children of Lesbians and Gays Everywhere (COLAGE) is a national organization just like Parents and Friends of Lesbians and Gays (PFLAG). When a friend's daughter went to college, she "came out" as the child of a lesbian in one of her women's studies courses and did a research paper in which she interviewed other children of lesbians and gays about their experience. The friends she made in that project stayed together for years. Another daughter of a lesbian went to college and was told by her classmates that she had to meet so-and-so because he had a queer dad. Comparing, discussing, and processing their experiences as children did form a bond. They became friends, then lovers. Both queer parents were at their wedding several years later, and the mother of the bride and her partner were escorted prominently down the church aisle by an usher. The groom's father left his beloved leather motorcycle jacket at home and appeared in a three-piece suit. My lover and I attended, as did several other lesbian couples who had been close to the bride during her growing-up years. All in all, it was a joyful occasion and an affirmation of how we have managed to make families for ourselves in spite of enormous barriers.

Lesbians have always had children. What is changing is how we are choosing those children and the contexts in which we are able to raise our children. When Ann had a daughter in 1952, the world was different than when Susan's son was born in 1984. Not perfect, but different. As lesbian parents, we are achieving a kind of critical mass. Lesbians who choose children today, whether by birth or adoption, are not alone. They are supported by community resources, by others who have gone before and not been closeted, and—I hope—by a community of lesbians who have not chosen children.

REFERENCES

1. *The New York Times*, December 2, 1992.
2. *Tucson Daily Star*, May 16, 1993.
3. Ibid.
4. *Times*, December 2, 1992.
5. Charlotte Patterson, "Children of the Lesbian Baby Boom," in Beverly Greene and Gregory Herek, ed., *Contemporary Perspectives on Gay and Lesbian Psychology*. Newbury Park, CA: Sage Publications, 1994.

6. *The New York Times*, September 8, 1993.

7. April Martin, *The Lesbian and Gay Parenting Handbook*. New York: Harper-Collins, 1993, pp. 131–34.

RESOURCES

Organizations:

COLAGE: Children of Lesbians and Gays Everywhere
(Sponsored by GLPCI: Gay and Lesbian Parents Coalition International)
P.O. Box 50360
Washington, DC 20091
202-583-8029
COLAGE sponsors an annual conference and publishes a quarterly newsletter for $5 (GLPCI).

Lesbian Mothers' National Defense Fund
Mom's Apple Pie
P.O. Box 21567
Seattle, WA 98111
206-325-2643

This group provides information and referrals to lesbians currently fighting custody cases. Also publishes a newsletter and a list of support groups.

The National Center for Lesbian Rights
870 Market Street, Suite 570
San Francisco, CA 94102
415-392-6257

The center also publishes the following information pamphlets:
AIDS and Child Custody: A Guide to Advocacy (1990)
A Lesbian and Gay Parents' Legal Guide to Child Custody (1989)
Lesbians Choosing Motherhood: Legal Implications of Donor Insemination and Coparenting (1991)
Lesbian Mother Litigation (1990)
Preserving and Protecting the Families of Lesbians and Gay Men (1990)

Books:

Laura Benkov, *Reinventing the Family*. New York: Crown, 1994. The emerging story of lesbian and gay parents—how they are challenging deeply held assumptions about family and creating new paradigms in an often hostile world.

April Martin, *The Lesbian and Gay Parenting Handbook*. New York: HarperCollins, 1993. An excellent resource, including sample donor-recipient and coparenting agreements and a donor screening form.

Louise Rafkin, *Different Mothers*. Pittsburgh: Cleis Press, 1990. Sons and daughters of lesbian mothers talk about their experiences growing up, their relationships with their mothers.

Kath Weston, *Families We Choose*. New York: Columbia University Press, 1991. A thought-provoking consideration of kinship. Includes sections on coming out, building gay families, parenting, and the politics of gay families.

PART SEVEN

Power Issues

Power and Mutuality

*I*n no relationship are we going to be equal in all things. There will always be something in which I am stronger, at which I am better, about which I know more. And the same is true for her. I expect to match her in some important things, but in other ways we adjust. My breath gives out sooner when we are climbing and Jan slows back for me. My legs are longer, so I let Jan lead the way when we are bicycling. I could leave her behind on the bicycle; I have the power to do that, but I don't like riding alone.

Power isn't always about physical strength. I played a team game not long ago in which my team had to move from the chalked squares we each stood in to the chalked squares occupied by the other team. The rules prohibited obvious solutions. Soon, one or two of my team members suggested a complex series of moves that would get each team to the others' places. Did I understand what was being proposed? Not for a minute. I put my trust in someone else's ability to do complex spatial analysis and moved exactly the way I was told to without understanding why. I trusted I would end up where they wanted me to be and that I would want to be where they wanted me to be.

That was a game and both teams won when we completed the task. We let the people who had the power of understanding this particular left-brain function take the lead. We do the same in life all the time, and frequently, as a result, both "teams" win. Sarah and Joline are both courageous women, but during their years together they've found the power of courage works for them differently. "When one of Sarah's sisters was arrested on a drug charge, and we thought the police had been worse than they ought to have been under the circumstances," remembers Joline with cautious understatement, "she couldn't talk about it. I wanted her to go to a lawyer, raise her voice, *do* something. I was so angry I could hardly stand it." What happened? Did Sarah speak out. "No," Joline shook her head. "She asked me to do it. And I didn't have any trouble at all. I knew Sylvia, her sister, and I went in there with a lawyer who was a friend of my father's and we raised high, holy hell." She smiles at the memory. "We were right, too. It was something that had to be done." Everyone benefited because Sarah knew what she couldn't do and Joline was willing to do what she knew she could.

Sarah's courage comes out, not in confrontation and rarely in words, but in actions. She is the woman who ran across six lanes of traffic, Joline tells me, to help a man whose car had caught fire after an accident. "I was driving," Joline remembers, "and I saw the accident and put on the brakes. I don't think our car had even stopped when I saw this tall blonde woman dodging cars to get to the other side of the highway. He'd gotten free of the car, but his clothes were burning. Several people were standing there, horrified, wondering what to do, when Sarah knocked him to the ground and started rolling over him to put out the fire. By the time I got across the road, it was all over." Joline says Sarah is the person she'd most like to have with her in a time of crisis. And Sarah says she relies on Joline "when somebody's got to be stood up to, confronted."

We call this back-and-forth sharing of power in a relationship mutuality. Mutuality is a function of our interdependence as human beings. No one person can live or function alone, in isolation. That is the human condition. When we volunteer to meet one another's needs and have ours met reciprocally, we say we are practicing mutuality. When one person forces others to serve his or her human needs, we say that person is a tyrant; the people who are trapped into serving are slaves or victims or servants or—sometimes—wives.

Mutuality in a relationship means that I am affecting her and being affected by her. Each of us is open to being touched by the other, to letting her have an impact on us—emotionally, physically, intellectually—in every way imaginable. We are mutually vulnerable and mutually responsible for the relationship, for one another, and for ourselves. Mutuality means that I am open to the possibility of changing, of becoming a different kind of person as a result of her influence, and she is open to the same. Mutuality cannot occur if one partner holds the power all the time in a relationship.

In some lesbian communities, mutuality has been misunderstood and labeled codependence. Many of us aren't sure what codependence is exactly, but we know it's supposed to be bad. "Oh, they're so codependent" is usually a statement of scorn or dismissal. Jan and I have heard it applied to our relationship, sometimes in a teasing tone of voice, but with an undertone that questions or criticizes. To revert to one scenario I mentioned earlier, when I make Jan's lunch for her because she goes out to work and I work at home, I'm not exhibiting symptoms of codependence but of mutuality. I like making her lunch for her, it is not an obligation, and the fact that I make her lunch does not limit her in any way.

Codependency means not making choices that please yourself. It means compromising yourself for another person. Because codependency has been misunderstood and misapplied, I think sometimes we are afraid to do something for someone else, even when we might want to.

One symptom or component of codependency is enabling. *Enabling* was originally applied to someone who assisted an alcohol or chemically dependent person in satisfying her addiction. If, instead of making Jan's lunch, I was going out and buying her liquor and delivering it to her at work so that she could continue a destructive habit, and if I did this because I was afraid of what might happen to me if I didn't, or if I did this because I wanted her to stay at work and not go spend the afternoon in a bar and get fired, then I think I would be acting in the realm of what was originally called enabling.

Other forms of enabling take place around obsessive behaviors that are harmful to an individual, behaviors like needing to be sexual with every woman you meet, like gambling, like overeating or starving. Minimizing the negative effects of such behaviors on a friend or lover—without confronting the behavior itself—is damaging in the long run.

But caring for one another in healthy and mutual ways is not something we should be labeling codependence. It is not about codependency, it is about love and mutuality.

Some power issues in relationships come about because one partner has more experience or knowledge than the other; some exist because society gives certain people more status. White people, Christian people, physically attractive or able-bodied people, for example, are all rewarded in this culture because of traits they did not earn. As a white woman, I cannot choose *not* to accept the status that comes with my skin color. I would have to change the bedrock on which this society operates in order to do that. I can change my own awareness of my white-skin privilege, my willingness to exploit it. I can work actively against this inequality. But if I, as a white woman, am in a relationship with a woman who is black or brown, we are going to have to deal with our power differences every time we go out in the world. And we can be sure they will filter into our home as well.

Mutuality, in all of these circumstances, only works if both partners are conscious of the issues *and* are aware of their own strengths and weaknesses. True mutuality requires that each of us function from strength, not weakness.

Defining the Norm

Some status symbols in this culture will never change, at least not in several lifetimes more than any one of us will get to live. Race—white is dominant. Class—upper or at least middle is dominant. Religion—it's cool to acknowledge the "Judeo-Christian" heritage of the United States, but the norm is Christian, period. And so is able-bodied. We can measure our distance from the norm by how many adjectives precede the noun. An astronaut? Or a female astronaut? Or a Jewish female astronaut?

Joan is a feminist. I am a lesbian feminist. My friend Bernice is a Jewish lesbian feminist. My friend Barbara is a black lesbian feminist. Joan never thinks to describe herself as a white, heterosexual, able-bodied, Christian feminist, although that would be an accurate account of her point of view. I try, but do not always remember, to say that I am a white and able-bodied as well as a lesbian feminist. It matters most when I use the word *we* to describe lesbians in a certain way. Do I mean all lesbians? Or do I mean white lesbians? Or lesbians who can see, hear, walk?

When parts of our self-definition are incorporated into the norm, we don't have to think about them. In fact, we are encouraged not to think about them. In a workshop I have led called "Defining the Norm," one exercise is to divide the group into heterosexuals and homosexuals. They face each other across the room and I ask them what they would want to say to these people apart from them who represent the "other." If individuals in the group know and trust one another, some interesting things are usually said. Then I ask the bisexuals from each side of the room to come to the center and stand between the homosexuals and the heterosexuals. On one occasion, one woman from the homosexual group came to the center and two men and a woman from the heterosexual side came to the center. As they approached one another, the heterosexual woman said to the lesbian, "But that isn't fair. You can't be in two groups."

I was thrilled, of course, at this demonstration. The heterosexual woman had just defined one of the predominant characteristics of the norm: it doesn't exist. She didn't think heterosexuals were a group, hence when she went to the bisexual group, it was her "first" group. The lesbian had one group definition—homosexual—and was trying to take on a second.

Heterosexuals may not think of themselves as having a preference, but their response to learning that they do is usually fairly mild or benign.[1] I am always surprised—in contrast—when I do this workshop and remember how angry white people get when we are required to define ourselves as white. "I don't think of myself that way" is one of the most common reasons I hear, "so why are you trying to label me?" Of course we don't think of ourselves as white. That is one of the privileges of being the norm. When I divide a group into "white" and "other" I always have to send some people back to the white side. Sometimes Italians ("I'm Mediterranean"), sometimes the Irish ("We're Celtic"), sometimes "I'm not white, I'm just an American." Right. It would be nice. When Jewish people go to the "other" side or stay on the white side, we have interesting discussions about the differences between race and ethnicity and culture. "Why are Catholics white," one participant wanted to know, "when Jews aren't?" Another man whose father is Mexican and mother is from the United States was challenged by the "other" group to come and join them. "Why?" he asked. "My father's people came from Spain. It may have been four hundred years ago, but we're white."

The most serious issue for me in this segment of the workshop is not to define who is white and who is not, but to help white people understand that white is not a color, it is a privilege. We *are* white, whether we like it or not, and feeling guilty about that or angry at those who tell us we *are* white isn't very useful. Nor is the assertion "But I didn't do it," or "It wasn't my ancestors, we weren't here yet." For all white people, there are historical reasons to be ashamed of our race. We aren't unique in that, as a race, by the way, we just happen to be the most recent and most dominant norm race. For some white people, there are more immediate and personal reasons for our guilt and anger. But until we can move from reactive emotions to more positive actions to correct injustice, to create justice, we only perpetuate the norm of racism and white privilege.

Defining the norm in terms of class privilege can be complicated in a different way. Many people feel they began life in one class and then moved up or slid down into another. Unlike racial definitions, class mythology in this country expounds a certain mobility. Frequently, workshop participants define their "class of origin" differently from their current class status. "I'm definitely lower class," asserted one young man proudly. "Then who," I asked him, "paid for those braces on your teeth?" His orthodontia was impressive and looked quite expensive. "Oh," he said, embarrassed, "my grandmother." He may not have any money of his own now, but he is attached to money.

Many who do this workshop act as though they had quickly and easily shed all of the attitudes, ideals, and skills that came with a certain class status. We've all known someone or read an article about someone who was alive during the Great Depression and is still living as though prosperity were momentary, as though every scrap of food had to be eaten, every penny saved. Why are the habits of being middle class or upper class any less ingrained? Why are the skills of making every penny count more likely to stay with us than, say, the skills gained in an expensive education? They aren't. Nor are the teeth that were cared for and straightened by expensive orthodontia

going to suddenly develop an excessive overbite because we're grocery shopping on a tight budget and can't afford to eat in a restaurant
even once a month.

Race and class of origin are not matters we have control over. We
are born into a family. When we react with shame or pride to a historical accident, says activist Bernice Mennis,

> that blame or credit often prevents us from seeing clearly the
> actual effects of growing up in a certain class: what it allows,
> what it inhibits, blocks, destroys. Also, if we take credit for what
> is out of our control, we sometimes do not take sufficient credit
> and responsibility for what is in our control: our consciousness,
> our actions, how we shape our lives.[2]

Defining the norm, finding those parts of ourselves that we hadn't
named because they were normal and not "other," is a useful exercise
for couples because the differential between the norm and other is
usually about power. And if we are unconscious about differences in
power, if we use them to our advantage without realizing they exist,
they skew relationships. Unacknowledged power differences in a relationship can tie the relationship up in knots. Or tear it apart.

So? We're in love. We're both women. How can any of these other
differences matter?

Race and Class

Y ou got it," Mariana assures me when I ask her about race differences in her relationship. "I may be a Latina, but I'm light-skinned. That's always going to make it easier for me than it is for Lisa."

I'm surprised and say so. I thought that cultural differences would matter more than race. Mariana may be light-skinned, but she could not pass for white in this culture. "It doesn't matter," she assures me. "Our landlord, the clerk at the convenience store when I go in late, the old lady downstairs—she knows us both, but when Lisa comes up behind her on the porch, she's afraid. She's not afraid of me. I know that." The fact that Mariana has a level of comfortableness (I can think of no other word to describe this result of racism) in her life out in the world that is unavailable to Lisa does affect their relationship, even though they are aware of the dynamic.

"It's pretty subtle in some ways," Lisa says. "Mariana and I both love to go north in the fall and see the leaves changing color. We try to go for a weekend. It's our time together—and neither of us grew up in this part of the country, so we're pretty awed, moved, I guess, by being outdoors, seeing the color. But every year I want to go and I don't want to go."

I know what she's talking about. Vermont, New Hampshire, the Adirondacks are not known for their large populations of African Americans. "We walk into a restaurant in one of those small towns and everyone turns to stare. Now I know staring at strangers is a national pastime in small towns. But this is different. I have to worry about maybe they aren't just staring, maybe they're either hostile or afraid." I can see that this would inhibit Lisa's sense of freedom, destroy the emotional opening that she and Mariana might be sharing on their special weekend. Doesn't it affect Mariana too, I ask? "Of course," Lisa says, surprised at my question. "She wants to protect me. I want to protect her. Sometimes I pretend I don't see it, but you can't just make it go out of your mind. So I'm pretending it's not there and she's hoping I haven't noticed it, and our spontaneity gets a little stifled." An understatement if I ever heard one.

"Some of our white friends have said they experience the same thing because they're two women together," Mariana inserts. "But it isn't the same thing. You can choose your discretion level if you're a white lesbian and think people are looking at you weird. Like you can't snuggle, or hold hands at dinner, or have intense conversations and gaze into one another's eyes, you know what I mean?" I do, but I'm not sure I agree. Homophobia is real and so is racism. One doesn't diminish the other.

"Of course it doesn't," agrees Deborah, who lives in Washington, D.C., with her lover, Peggy. "I'm uncomfortable being black at most lesbian events and being gay at most black events, but, hey, you learn to cope." What does coping mean to a relationship, I want to know? "Coping means knowing how the world is and knowing what's most important to you and getting it however you can," she says without hesitation. Right. Is that easier with a lover of the same race? "Sure," she says, laughing. "I was with a couple of white women when I was younger. They were nice, you know, but I'd wake up in the morning and see this white face lying on the pillow next to me. No matter how much I liked her, she wasn't family. And I wanted a lover who was family. Bottom line."

Sarah, who is white, and Joline, who is black, have lived together as lovers, as family, for twenty years. They aren't out to most of their extended families, but two of Joline's sisters know that Jo and Sarah are "more than friends." The things that came up for them around race, insists Jo, "we mostly dealt with when we were in junior high school. You know, the bad language, the taunts." "Remember the time one of the boys called you a faggot?" Sarah asked. "He wanted something bad . . . " "Right," Jo agrees, "and he was afraid to use *nigger* and he hadn't learned *dyke* or *bull dagger* yet."

What about now? It's not much of an issue, they agree together. Jo is a respected professional, a nurse/supervisor at a large teaching hospital. Sarah's paid work is at a grocery store, but her real work is done at home alone. She's beginning to get quite a reputation as a cake baker and decorator, creative work she loves and can be proud of. Their few friends have always known them together and don't expect anything else, and they don't socialize at all out in public. Vacations consist of a week in the summer at Provincetown with a group of friends. If they wanted more, demanded more, perhaps they'd experience problems, either in the world or between themselves. But for now, they've achieved a balance they're comfortable with, a balance that works for them, and the world isn't too important.

All three of these couples are from the same class background in their families of origin, even if their incomes today vary somewhat, particularly those of Joline and Sarah. In fact, all of the nine sample couples except Wanda and Kathryn are from similar class situations, a fact I had not expected, given their other diversities. And when I initially talked with Wanda and Kathryn, the potential difficulties they were dealing with in their therapy seemed to have everything to do with the enormous changes they were contemplating: living together, living on Kathryn's salary while Wanda went back to school, moving to wherever Wanda was accepted at medical school, and so on. Not really, they told me a few months later.

"I guess I was so afraid of Wanda's being dependent on my salary because I saw my dad never being able to earn enough to let us be really comfortable," Kathryn said. "And I guess I was a little jealous. If there'd been any money, any way for me to fund it, I would have gone to medical school. I was smart in the right way. A couple of boys who were my buddies in high school science classes—they aced spots at great colleges and went straight to med school. I had to work part time and put myself through a community-college physical-therapy program. It was as close as I could come." After two years of training, Kathryn was a physical-therapy assistant and had worked long enough to be able to complete her advanced p.t. training. "I just finished paying for me to go to school, and then there's this thing Wanda wants and I love her and say, 'Sure, why not, honey,' but she picks up that somewhere, deep inside, I'm freaking."

What was your first clue? I ask Wanda. "No sex." She laughs, then admits, "Not really. I just felt some tension between us and I didn't know what it was, so when we were in one of our therapy sessions—because we both felt safe there—I just started pushing to find out what it was." It was in that session that they began to understand what the class difference meant to them in their couple dynamic.

"I didn't finish college because it didn't really matter. I knew if I wanted it later, it would be there for me. We had money. Lots of money. My dad was a bank CEO. We skied at Vail every winter, took vacations out of the country whenever he had the time. And then it was gone." Gone? Wanda nods. "Every bit of it. The bank failed, the money was gone, the house was gone, the boat was gone—for a while we thought Dad might be going to prison, but that didn't happen, thank God—and there I was, still thinking I might finish college someday." She laughs, but it isn't funny.

I'm beginning to see the dynamic. Wanda's assumption that Kathryn could, and would, support her came from old expectations. And Kathryn's feeling that she couldn't really do it, no matter how much she wanted to, came from her own old expectations.

"We haven't changed our plans," Kathryn tells me. "But we've figured out some new ways of going about it. We're talking more about what it means. And that I don't have to be the only one responsible for us financially. If something goes wrong, well, Wanda will work a bit too." Wanda agrees. "I've waited this long. It wouldn't be any big deal. It's a big deal that we're both doing what we want to do." For Wanda and Kathryn, new knowledge about their differences has helped untie the knot that might have kept them from going forward together.

Body Image and Disability

*L*isa is a large woman. "In addition to being black and six feet tall in my stocking feet," she says, "I weigh 235 pounds. There's a lot of me." She moves like a cat, smooth and self-assured, and she carries herself with all of the air and confidence of a beautiful woman. Because she is beautiful. But so are many large women who do not think of themselves that way, who have been unable to overcome the social stereotypes of thin and diminutive as beautiful. "I look like all the women in my family," Lisa tells me. "Every one of them, my great-grandma on down. Six feet and zaftig." I raise an eyebrow at her use of a Yiddish word to describe herself. "You know," she laughs again, "strong and *womanly*. I wasn't raised to think I was fat."

Fat. There's that word. To most women it's one of the ugliest words in the English language. If we didn't already know it, *The New England Journal of Medicine* has weighed in with an editorial announcing that discrimination against fat people "is the last fashionable form of prejudice." Recent studies published in that journal and elsewhere confirm that women who are fat (officially defined for us as "the top 5% of people on an index in which weight is related to height") are less likely to marry and far, far more likely to be poor.[3]

"I know that," says Lisa impatiently. "It's ridiculous. If I were five foot five and weighed a hundred pounds less, I'd be in a job that paid twice as much—some highly visible job instead of working nights as a temp doing data entry for a law firm. It's not that I don't have the skills."

"Don't get us started," suggests Mariana ominously, and I can tell that this is a subject they have worried frequently. But I want them to talk for this record, and they have no problem doing that. "It's the sickest thing imaginable," fumes Mariana. "Someone at the employment agency told Lisa that if she lost sixty pounds and paid some money up front to have breast-reduction surgery . . . " Her voice starts to slide up the scale. "Imagine it. Breast reduction. That she could earn twice as much as she's earning now."

Lisa and Mariana and I all know the statistics about women mutilated by body-image surgery, women starved by diets until their bodies are damaged, hearts worn out by yo-yo weight loss and gain. Mariana has a new one. "I heard last week that they did a study of Miss America contestants." Yes? That timeless image of American female beauty? "In the last thirty years, the average weight of Miss America contestants has gone down something like twenty-five pounds." She pauses and I sense this is not all. "*And* she's several inches taller." Which means that the ideal of female beauty in this country (if we let advertising and marketing imagery decide that for us) is very similar to the body type of an adolescent male.[4]

"Figures," snorts Lisa in disgust. "They'll let us into the job market but we have to look like boys."

"I guess that's true," agrees Ann slowly when I ask her about her impressions. "But I've only been paying attention to this weight thing in the last ten years. When I was working and raising my daughter and riding horses every day, well, I never thought about my weight, and it never seemed to change. Now," she looks down at her ample waist and hips, "well, Margaret says there's more of me to love."

Ann's weight may not bother her lover, Margaret, but I can tell Ann is not comfortable with it. I remember when I asked her to describe making love with Margaret for the first time. I was most focused on how Ann dealt with the loss of her breast to a mastectomy and the resulting scars. It was she who mentioned her spare tires around the middle. "Yes," she agrees when I ask her about it. "This extra weight bothers me more than only having one breast. That's a fact."

Kathryn understands what Ann is talking about. "I suffered through high school without a perfect body. Everybody around me was dating or at least doing athletics. Or at least cheerleading." She laughs at the latter. Not only did Kathryn have a severe curvature of the spine, called scoliosis, as a child, but during those impossibly difficult teen years she wore under her clothes a body brace that held her spine rigid and made her look as if she weighed thirty pounds more than she did. "Dating wasn't one of the options while I was wearing that thing," she says, "so I missed whatever it was that other kids my age were learning. But I learned some much harder things." Among the lessons Kathryn learned was that the condition over which she had no control was somehow shameful. "Everybody talked about it as 'your problem.' Nobody ever said what it was. For years I was ashamed, as though by not being good enough or smart enough, I'd caused my own deformity." She says the word *deformity* bitterly.

Today, Kathryn can swim, dance, hike, bicycle—most of the activities she loves. She notices that she fatigues quickly if she plays tennis too long, and she's been told that jogging is not a good idea for her. But she isn't terribly limited in what she can do by the curvature of her spine. The brace held the development of the curve to a minimum until her bones were finished growing. "And I was lucky, as these things go," she says. "My curvature was an 'S' curve. I matched on the top and bottom so my shoulders stayed pretty straight. Some people with a 'C' curve, it's much more obvious."

As a result, Kathryn has what is referred to as a "hidden disability," one that is affecting her but pretty much unknown to a casual observer. She doesn't feel her disability particularly affects her relationship with Wanda. Kathryn is much more aware of other attitudes toward her body and sexuality, attitudes that were a result of being raised in a fundamentalist Christian home, attitudes she has been changing since she became aware of them.

Some hidden disabilities do affect individuals more profoundly:

severe arthritis, chronic fatigue syndrome, diabetes, epilepsy, heart disease, among others, and some forms of surgery, like a colostomy (attaching the colon to a bag for elimination). When we act as though everyone were able-bodied, because we cannot "see" a disability in the group we are addressing, we may be forgetting these individuals.

Deafness is a disability that can be unnoticed at first. Beth has some small amount of residual hearing at certain frequencies, but prefers generally not to use a hearing aid. "It just amplifies sounds that don't make any sense," she explains. "So people don't see me coming in the same way they do a person in a wheelchair or using a cane." At work as a legal secretary, Beth interacts only with those who know she is deaf, rather than with the general public. "I suppose I'd make a sign or something in a situation like that," she says, laughing. "You know, DEAF PERSON AT WORK, DON'T SHOUT, I CAN'T HEAR YOU. I don't know why, but hearing people seem to get so angry at deaf people, like we aren't hearing what they have to say on purpose."

Beth says she is fairly unusual among deaf people. Because she lost her hearing after she learned to speak, her language skills remain fairly high. And her parents were fairly radical for their time, insisting that Beth learn to sign in A.S.L. as well as learn to read English and keep up her work with spoken language. "Sandra's daughter Megan won't have as easy a time with speech as I've had," she explains, "since she's never heard how a human voice ought to sound."

Sandra and Beth agree that Beth's disability—they are both comfortable calling her hearing loss that—does affect their relationship, but they aren't sure how. "I wouldn't say it causes a power imbalance between us," says Beth, in response to my question, "because we are both committed to doing whatever it takes so that I can communicate. And so that Megan will be able to communicate."

They know there are some things they have to work at harder than other couples might—making sure that things are clear between them, for example. "I'm decent at signing now," Sandra maintains, "but not sophisticated, even after six or so years of study. I have to be careful not to take shortcuts, not to say, 'Oh, never mind,' when I do mind." Beth's sense of carefulness is around not relying too much on Sandra's ears. "When we go out with friends, I have to make sure I'm interacting with them, not letting Sandra do the work and then asking her to tell me about it. But at the same time I have to say I rely on her ability to get all of the details so that we can hash things out later." Sandra laughs. "I may get the spoken details, but you should be around for one of our debriefings some night. Beth knows things from watching people's faces and body language that I miss entirely. Putting it all together *is* fun."

And both women are aware that Sandra's decisions about her daughter Megan are hers to make. "But if I ignored what Beth knows and has experienced," she says, "that would be really stupid. Beth has so much to teach me. And Megan. Being with her is a gift I never dreamed of when I first learned that Megan couldn't hear."

What Sandra and Beth are describing, I think, is the kind of mutuality I described earlier. Each has recognized her own strength or power and that of her partner; this recognition allows them to give the other help when it's needed without feeling resentful, pushed aside, or guilty.

I've Lived Longer Than You (and Learned More)

I'm not sure living longer equates with learning more," Susan says, "but I think it's a myth a lot of us believe." Susan is ten years younger than her lover, Barbara. When they met—at twenty-eight and thirty-eight—the ten years seemed significant, partly because Barbara's daughter was an independent ten-year-old and Susan was just contemplating starting a family. "Barbara had already been through most of the things I was just facing—getting a divorce, having a child, figuring out my work life. I think we both assumed she knew more than me about those things. I relied on her and she expected to be able to give me advice. That gave her a lot of power in our relationship."

What was the effect of that, I want to know, and how did they deal with it? "It took us a while to notice it," Susan confesses, "but I think it became significant when I began to want to do some things for myself, my own way. Barbara thought she already knew how to do it and I'd hear a lot about what was the point of reinventing the wheel?" But those situations are never really the same, I point out, unlike the knowledge and skill required to change a flat tire or roast a perfect turkey.

"Right. That's what we discovered. My divorce wasn't the same as hers. My husband wasn't abusive and we didn't have a child. Barbara wanted me to take precautions that were unnecessary. Not to mention we didn't have the money to pay a lawyer. My pregnancy wasn't even the same as hers. She didn't have *any* morning sickness." She underlines the word *any* with disgust. "I vomited every morning for three months. And I thought she ought to be able to tell me what to do about it." She's laughing now at the memory, at how silly it seems, but the expectation was obviously difficult for them at the time.

Barbara is smiling too, and waves a hand in the air for emphasis. "I thought she needed advice. I'd wake up and find popcorn or cracker crumbs on my pillow. She was eating in the middle of the night so she wouldn't ever have an empty stomach." She shook her head. "None of it helped, but you can see why I thought she might need advice.

"When we changed our attitudes—I mean, when I changed my attitude—" Barbara hastens to correct herself, "was when we decided to go into business together. Susan had to learn it all, not rely on me. She had to learn it well enough to be able to do it and make decisions about a job. She couldn't just be my assistant carpenter." Why not, I ask. There is silence for a moment. "Well, it just seemed like Susan wanted the skills so she could be on her own if she ever needed to be." I know they are referring to the fact that today Barbara has ovarian cancer. But when they began the business five years ago, both women were healthy. Susan sees my question. "I needed the autonomy," she says. "I didn't mind us being in business together, but I couldn't imagine us working the same jobs every day and then going home and basically spending every minute of every day together. I think that destroys relationships."

Today, at thirty-nine and forty-nine, Susan and Barbara don't feel their age difference the way they did eleven years ago. Part of that is due to their life circumstances and part to the conscious work they put into dealing with this issue when it came up in their relationship.

I asked Ann, who is retired now, whether age had made a difference when she lived with a woman much younger, whether she felt more in control of the relationship as a result of her experience.

"Of course age made a difference," Ann says loudly, her body language assertive, "but not like you're saying. It's the younger one who has the power. She's more attractive. She has more options. Nancy was thirteen years younger than me, and she left me for a woman her own age. I was in my fifties and not hip enough for her, I guess." I agree the difference between the late thirties and the early fifties can be quite a gap, but I thought Ann had said she broke up with Nancy because of Nancy's drinking. "Well, sure, that was part of it," Ann agrees. "But we wanted different things, too. She wanted excitement, the chance to travel. I wanted to have a home that was secure and to finish raising my girl." She shrugs. "Maybe the drinking wouldn't have been so bad if I'd wanted to go out to the clubs and things with her."

I'm skeptical about that, but listen to what Ann is saying. "We were at different stages in our lives, basically. I'm not saying it can't work with a younger woman, but I think we all pretty much want similar things at similar ages. Nancy has settled down now that she's fifty—she's got a home, a partner, lots of dogs and cats. She wants now what I wanted then. Now I want to travel more, since I'm free of the responsibility for my daughter."

Power differences may be real when they are based on age and experience, but they are also shifting. As our ages change, so do our abilities and our desires. What matters at one age may not matter at another. Society may give more status to maturity when it is compared to immaturity, but Ann is also right—youth and beauty are powerfully supported status symbols.

The Trouble Is We Don't Understand One Another

*I*n her book *We Say We Love Each Other*, poet Minnie Bruce Pratt shows two women together in their home. One goes to answer the phone, talks for a moment, then comes back into the room where her lover sits. Her lover does not ask, Who called? To her, such a question would be an intrusion. The woman who answered the phone is hurt. To her, the failure to inquire is a failure of closeness, of caring. As Pratt looks at the two women (the first herself) sitting on the couch, the space of their whole lives between them, she explains:

> I am sitting in a place made for me
> by women, generations, Scot, Irish, sitting
> on a little bit of land, holding on,
> survival on an island, isolation, a closed mouth
> in their own kitchen, self-containment.
>
> You are sitting in a place made for you
> by women, generations, Jews in Spain, Holland,
> Russia, the Pale, Poland, Roumania, America,
> the pogroms, no bit of land safe, none

to be owned as home, survival by asking, asking,
knowing where every one was, enemy, family.[5]

Ethnic differences, like the ones Pratt is exploring in this poem, are shaped by generations of cultural expectations. They affect all of us, and many times ethnic diversity is a source of joy and strength in the life of a couple. When we don't understand the nature of our differences, however, it can lead to anger, bitterness, accusations of being uncaring, when in fact just the opposite is being expressed— but the way it is being expressed is unrecognized.

Ethnic differences may include political differences, but not always, and they are not the same. I have two friends, a couple, who are Israeli Jewish and Lebanese Christian. They differ politically on many things, but culturally they have more in common with each other than the woman who is a Lebanese Christian has with me, who was raised a Christian in this North American culture.

Cultural or ethnic differences only become power issues if one or both lovers assume that one way of being is more "right" than the other. In the scenario described by Minnie Bruce Pratt, for example, I can imagine the lover who expects to be asked who called on the telephone telling her partner that it is healthier to be more open in their intimate relationship, less private, less secret. If my lover said that to me, my immediate response would be to become defensive. "You think you're healthier than me?" I would probably ask belligerently, ready for a fight. I would *not* be ready to explore our cultural differences. And I would have a right to question my lover's assumption. Intimacy does not depend on knowing every detail of one another's lives; and while intimacy is nurtured by openness, we usually mean emotional openness when we speak of this, not a more casual knowing of details.

What makes us able—and willing—to explore our differences without judgment? Usually, the ability I mentioned earlier, the ability to not take credit or blame for things over which we have no control. We are born into a cultural context, just as we are born into a race and class. That we are shaped by that culture as children growing up is inevitable. As adults, we can look at the traits and habits that come with that culture and decide which are serving us well and which are not. That we have grown up a certain way should not be the issue; how we take responsibility for our own growth and happiness is what is important.

Beneath the obvious power differences that a couple might encounter—if one is African American and the other white, or if one is Jewish and the other Christian, or any variety of other power differences that result from the hierarchical structures under which we live—are also cultural differences. To be African American is a cultural identity in this country as well as a racial identity. Cultural differences ought to be just that: differences. Unfortunately, we value some cultures more than others, not always consistently either, and so a feature of human identity that ought to be exciting, fun, and benign can become a power issue.

Marty, the ex-nun, who lived on a farm with Joan, the ex-corporate businesswoman, never expected that cultural differences would affect her relationship. "My whole name is Maria Regina Caprietti. If you wonder why I became a nun at the age of eighteen, the answer is there in my name, in my family's expectations of what at least one or two girls in a family of seven children, four girls, would grow up to be." Did being from an extended Italian family, where no one in the generations before you had ever married outside of that identification, carry more expectations than the obligation to dedicate some of the children to the church? I'm asking the obvious, as I can tell from her grimace. "Sure, but I didn't know that," she concludes simply.

And what about Joan? Joan Adams. Same class, lower middle, same race, same religion. "Well, sort of," says Marty, "though it's hard for me to think of Catholics and Presbyterians as the same religion, but I know what you mean." So was there a problem?

Yes, after all the other factors were sifted out, including their increasing use of alcohol as the years went by, there were problems. They noticed it first in how they dealt with anger. "I emoted and she stuffed." That's Marty's thumbnail sketch. "I know it isn't *only* about our cultural backgrounds, but it sure starts there. My anger seemed normal to me, like my mother's, you know? It scared Joan to death. Not that she'd admit that, of course, not at the time."

Joan had never heard either of her parents raise their voices in argument. "I thought screaming meant bad things. Like people who screamed at one another were expressing hatred. And were about to start hitting." Joan remembers the first time Marty was angry at her. "I was astonished. I'd heard her tell other people off—like a clerk at the grocery store who was being incredibly stupid—but I never thought she'd do it to me." What was the issue? "Do you know, I can't remember. All I can remember is how surprised and hurt I was. And, well, scared, too."

Joan had been taught that such expressions of anger were inappropriate and harmful. Marty had been taught that they were a normal part of family life, that angry confrontations were respectful and healthy. "After a while," Marty admits, "I began to think that Joan didn't really like me that much. She wouldn't engage with me." And Joan? "How could someone say they loved you and then scream at you like that? How could I believe she really cared for me, the real me?"

I know couples who have differences in how they express their anger or their love for whom those differences are like the bubbles in champagne—a pleasant tickle. Joan and Marty, however, were isolated in their relationship and in their rural lesbian community. They never considered asking for help outside the community, from a therapist, for example, and the other couples in their community didn't have experiences that could help them. Instead, their drinking escalated. Joan found that drinking helped her hide her fear. Marty's drinking tamped down her anger, which, she could tell, seriously upset Joan. They thought they were coping, but they never learned to appreciate their differences, and the relationship could not survive.

By These Hands—Betrayal

Domestic violence. How I wish those words had no place in a book about lesbian couples. We call it the second closet, a taboo of silence that hurts victims and does not help perpetrators. We keep the silence out of a misguided sense of community necessity. Wouldn't it just add fuel to the fires of homophobia if we admitted that lesbian relationships might be less than perfect? if we acknowledged that sometimes violence enters our homes also? But by keeping the silence we betray those women in our communities who need our help and comfort when they have been victims of battering. And by keeping the silence we betray our community. It is, after all, a community responsibility to say to women who use violence that this is not an option—not so that we can drum them out of the lesbian community for their "political incorrectness" but so that we can insist they find help.

On one occasion I was in the position of sponsor (friendly counselor) to a woman who was recovering from long-term alcohol and drug abuse. I discovered, after many months of long talks, that she was involved in physical abuse in her relationship with her lover and that she was the batterer. She was tormented by that fact, by the realization that this method of alleged "problem solving" was so ingrained in her from childhood that even when sober she couldn't seem to control her behavior. I was upset too. Physical abuse was not part of my childhood; it flies in the face of every value I've cultivated as an adult. And yet I had made a commitment to this woman, to keep talking with her as she struggled daily in her efforts to stay sober.

I solved my personal conflict by being very clear with her about my own values. We set limits on what could happen within the relationship, limits she tried very hard to honor. And she sought professional counseling to help her unlearn violence as a solution to her problems. The lover relationship ended fairly soon. The counseling continued. The behavior she hated changed. Battering does not have to be a part of our lives, no matter what we experienced as children, no matter what our previous learning has been. But the change can only happen when we acknowledge the problem, confront the behavior, connect to the pain that behavior is causing us, and desire the change.

Several different mind-sets conspire to keep lesbian domestic violence in the closet. One is the myth we sometimes embrace that says two women together share a bond that is deeper than that between a man and a woman. We know each other better, our intimacy is more profound, and therefore violence between us is unthinkable. The conclusion in that sequence obviously doesn't work, because whatever we may believe or wish to believe about the "specialness" of lesbian relationships, violence is, in fact, a reality. According to *Newsweek*, the Victim Recovery Program at Boston's Fenway Community Health Center was established in 1986 to aid victims of gay bashing. Today, half the phone calls received at the center concern domestic violence, many of them from lesbians.[6]

Another myth about domestic violence is that it is perpetrated by men against women. Or by men against men. How could a woman do that? But *that* is not a function of gender, it is a statement about power within a relationship, about a power inequity within a relationship. Power inequities, as I have been discussing in other contexts, are not uncommon, even in a relationship between two women. Not all power inequities result in physical violence, of course, but it is the inequity that allows violence in some cases. In other scenarios, violence is used to create a power difference, to give one partner control over the other's behavior by the threat or fact of violence.

When Sarah heaved the plate at Joline as she came through the door after her "date" with a man, Sarah couldn't really distinguish between a desire to hurt Joline for hurting her and a desire to simply get Joline's attention so that they could talk about what was happening. "I'm glad I didn't hurt her," Sarah reflects, "but like I said before, I don't ever want to get to that place where all I can do is strike out. I want to be able to talk about it earlier."

Sarah was also using physical violence to make her equal again in the relationship. Joline, by virtue of her professional status and income, was then in a dominant position, a position Sarah had been accustomed to holding for a while because she was three years older than Jo. By their mid-twenties, Sarah's age no longer gave her status. When Joline decided to go to the movies with a man, Sarah felt her own powerlessness reinforced; and so she heaved the plate to regain some power. Today, she's learned other ways to keep power in the relationship in balance. "I'm more soft-spoken than Jo," Sarah admits, "and I don't do as well in public. She's the lively one. I worked with a therapist for a while to be able to recognize first *when* I want something different from Jo and then how to tell her what I want." She laughs, a little embarrassed. "That may not seem like a lot to you, but for me—well, it wasn't something I learned in my family, how to ask for what I wanted. So doing it now is a big deal."

Of course it is a big deal. Anything that establishes us as equals in our relationships is important. And stabilizing.

Finally, violence in lesbian relationships can be a reflection of the larger society's homophobia—those messages we cannot help but absorb: homosexuals are sick, disgusting, how could two women do that? if God had meant . . . and so on. My own internalized homophobia has leaped out and grabbed me at times. I work hard against allowing those messages space in my psyche, but even with awareness, they occasionally slip past me.

Why does any woman stay in a brutal or damaging relationship?

Because she is convinced she does not deserve anything better. Heterosexual? lesbian? The messages might be different, but the denigration is the same.

What is to be done? Lesbians must be clear that we do not condone violence. And when I say violence, I do not mean anger, or s/m sex play, or wrestling in bed, or even naked antagonism and aggression on the rugby field or basketball court. I mean violence—behavior that is meant to physically hurt another person. We must understand ourselves—and be sure that every lesbian we know understands—what violence is and that violence is not an option in our personal relationships.

We must also be clear that no victim of violence "brings it on herself." No matter how enraging a partner's behavior might be, violence is not an acceptable response. Anger is. Even fury. Not violence.

I know how hard it can be to separate anger and violence. I've been enraged to the point of near irresponsibility. I've seen a look of fear on a lover's face, fear of my rage, fear that I might be violent. I never have struck a lover, and I never want to see that look of fear again.

Violence destroys trust and mutuality in a relationship, and when there is no trust or mutuality, intimacy dies. Without intimacy, there can be no "lover" relationship. Violence is not an expression of the extremity of our love; it is the failure of that love.

Daphne mistook violence for love, at least for a while. "I thought Sheila's jealousy was kind of neat at first. I'd never had anybody who seemed to care for me that much. She wanted to know everything about where I'd gone during the day, you know, who I'd had lunch with, that sort of thing." One night when Daphne was tired, she told Sheila she didn't want to talk right then and went into the bedroom to read a mystery. Sheila didn't follow her into the bedroom right away, but when she did, she was in a fury. "I've never been so surprised," Daphne says, "at least at one level. But you know, at another level, I guess I'd realized all along that I'd only be okay with her as long as I did exactly what she wanted."

I ask Daphne how long the violence went on, and she looks chagrined. "Too long," she says first, shaking her head. When I wait for more of an answer, she finally gives it. "I lived with that for nearly a year. Every time she hit me, she'd swear it would never happen again, that it was just that she loved me so much. Finally I realized being loved that much might get me killed. One night after we'd been out dancing, she accused me of looking at the bartender—you know, flirting. I mean, I hadn't even noticed the bartender. Sheila had gone to get the drinks. When I started, just started, to say that, she grabbed the china light by our bed and hit me over the head with it. There was glass everywhere. And blood. I got out of there by saying I needed to go to the emergency room. And I never went back. Not alone."

Daphne went to a friend's house that night. She'd heard of shelters for battered women, but never even thought of going there herself. "Battered women were heterosexual. Period. It wasn't something I could picture doing." Nor did she call the police. Both of these are options available to lesbians who are victims of abuse, although the laws vary from state to state. In some states, for example, domestic-violence laws protect only partners of the opposite sex. But other laws can protect lesbians—laws against assault, disorderly conduct, endangerment, imprisonment, kidnapping, trespassing, criminal damage, stalking, and use of the phone or mail to harass, threaten, or intimidate.

Daphne did call a lesbian therapist who advertised in the local lesbian newsletter. She'd copied the number out months before, when it became clear to her that Sheila's moods were more and more out of control. "I couldn't have gotten clear so quickly without her help," Daphne remembers. "It was fantastic to be able to talk to someone without having to explain something so basic about myself as that I was queer. It was hard enough to admit I'd let this woman hit me and push me around for a year. Under the circumstances, I couldn't have imagined talking to anyone but another lesbian."

Lesbians and Therapy

Many of the lesbians I know have been to a lesbian therapist, and, yes, some of my best friends are lesbian therapists. Nonetheless, I confess, I have never been to a lesbian therapist. When I have needed help in my life or in a relationship, the problem never seemed to be about "being" a lesbian, and so I never thought I needed a therapist who was a lesbian. I've seen two therapists about alcoholism, one when I thought I ought to, maybe, stop drinking, and one when I had quit and was trying to survive the experience. Years later I saw a counselor around some issues of grief. And most recently I've been fascinated by learning about family systems and how they affect me today. The counselors or therapists I sought out were all women, and that was not accidental. I feel safer with a woman. Why didn't I extend that and say I would feel safer with a lesbian?

At first, there were no lesbian therapists available where I lived and worked. Finding a woman therapist was a major achievement. When I did the grief therapy, I couldn't afford the lesbian therapists in my community and went to a social-services agency (there were then no acknowledged lesbians on this agency's staff) with a sliding-scale fee. And in the family-systems work, the sexual preference of the therapist seemed irrelevant to me; it happened that the person with the credentials to teach me what I wanted to learn was a heterosexual woman.

Friends have told me how important it was to them to have a lesbian therapist to talk with, especially when the issue was a relationship, and I do understand that. "It's just nice not to have to explain some things about a relationship," one friend told me, "like why your parents don't know and your partner's parents do know. That might be an issue, but a therapist who didn't understand closeting, or didn't understand my fear of homophobia, just wouldn't have cut it. She wouldn't have been useful." Couples who have gone into therapy together have been especially concerned to find a lesbian therapist. "There are so many givens you don't have to explain" was one woman's comment. Another friend said, "I didn't want her to try and fix me by making me heterosexual," reminding me that lesbians my age and older became adults in the fifties and sixties when therapy itself was often abusive—lesbians were thought to be sick, needed to be fixed. Some lesbians were traumatized by that kind of "therapy." One of my friends recalls her own well-meaning parent, who thought her daughter was too tomboyish and sent a sensitive thirteen-year-old to a psychiatrist who asked the child questions she didn't know the meaning of—but by which she was mortified and embarrassed.

When lesbians choose to go into therapy as adults, we generally do it because something in our inner lives isn't working well, is giving us some discomfort, or at the very least is not helping us be the women we want to be. Of the lesbians whose stories appear in this book, every one of those who went into therapy said she did it to free herself, free herself from some pattern of behavior, some expectation, some limitation that was keeping her from living as fully as she knew she could.

When Barbara went into therapy after she responded to Susan's sexual overtures with fear and rigidity, a response she did not understand, she discovered that she had been sexually abused as a child. In therapy she worked to overcome those unconscious patterns of response and behavior that remained with her as an adult. One lesbian therapist has described this process as "wading through the old experiences and reattaching the anger to them." The goal is to put the anger where it belongs (on the events and experiences that caused it), rather than directing it at people and events in the present. And it is good that we should do this.

Anger can be tricky, however. Sarah went into therapy to help her find a better expression of her anger than throwing plates at Joline. But I want to know whether she also found permission to be angry at a homophobic and racist society that would keep her from valuing her relationship with Joline. Was Barbara able to be angry at the patriarchal structure that inhibits her freedom to choose her sexual expression as well as to be angry at the specific man who forced her sexually when she was a child?

Why does this matter to me?

As women, lesbians have a difficult history with anger. We aren't supposed to have any. It's not feminine, we've been told. I was in the audience at a poetry reading in the early seventies when poet Adrienne Rich was reading from some of her strong feminist, strongly angry poetry. After the reading, which had moved and inspired every woman in the audience, if I could judge from the faces around me, a man rose during the question-and-answer period. His question was about anger. Adrienne Rich's anger. Didn't she think, he insisted, that her anger was making her a less universal poet? Wasn't her anger obscuring her vision, distorting her worldview? "No," Rich retorted at once. "Like the famous poet William Blake, I believe my anger is visionary anger." The audience applauded explosively.

I still think about that answer when people tell me my anger is unattractive or debilitating. Anger is one of the causative forces in our lives. Anger is the recognition of injustice—not only of the unjust things that have happened to us personally but also of the more cosmic injustices; out of that larger anger comes our energy to work for change in our world. "Anger is loaded with information and energy," Audre Lorde reminds us. "Every woman has a well-stocked arsenal of anger potentially useful against those oppressions, personal and institutional, which brought that anger into being. Focused with precision it can become a powerful source of energy serving progress and change."[7]

My fear about therapy has been that it will diffuse our anger rather than help us put our anger where it belongs. Barbara did important work when she went into therapy to remember, to deal with, to transform her own experience of child abuse. That action, however, will not make child abuse in this culture disappear. She has broken the cycle in her own life—an essential beginning—but this does nothing about the system in which we all live, which is abusive to children when it refuses to adequately educate them, when it cancels programs for child nutrition and medical care, for example. These are conditions that deserve, require our anger.

Lesbian therapists tell me, however, that they cannot have a goal for a client's healing beyond the obvious one of achieving what she has come into therapy for. Their job requires advocating only for the client's goals. Marty, who went from being a teacher to being a therapist in the lesbian community, says that balancing being a member of the community and being a mentor or counselor for some women in that community can be quite a "high-wire job and sometimes you forget to string up the safety net." She confesses she sometimes wants to give a client a "swift kick" or tell her to "get a life and stop whining." She laughs. "Not really," she says, but I wonder.

"Look, I'm a feminist. I want everyone in this community to work for change—big change, cosmic changes. But my piece in this is rather small. If I can help a woman be a little more comfortable in her life, give her some space to move, then maybe she'll be able to look around her and see the world really is a bigger place." Marty sounds defensive, and I ask her what I've said that's upsetting. "You want Every Lesbian to take her anger out and change the world. I've seen too many lesbians who were furious, but they didn't know why. And you know what they were doing?" I shake my head, afraid to interrupt. "They're out there putting unconscious anger into politics. That's when we get the lesbian feminist collective that resembles a drunken-family script, complete with scapegoat and bully. Or we get one lesbian attacking another for no reason anyone can discern. We call it lateral hostility, but you want to bet she hasn't dealt with her anger at her mother?" I'm still shaking my head. I wouldn't bet.

It is good, I think—in considering the role of therapy and therapists and their relationship to power—to remember that we have power in different ways in different arenas. Self-empowerment can be the goal of therapy, for client and therapist alike. Political goals, of necessity, are different. Politically, we want to empower our community through civil and legal rights, and these two arenas are interactive in every sense. As we strive for those rights, we hope that our actions will be guided by conscious rather than unconscious motives. Guaranteeing that consciousness is the responsibility of each of us, not just one group within our community.

Accountability

When Jan and I decided to have a commitment celebration, part of our impulse was to say to our friends, We're serious about this relationship and we want you to witness our commitments to one another and, if necessary, help us to keep them. We wanted to be held accountable to one another by ourselves and by our community.

I had then only a vague sense of what that accountability might mean for us as lesbians. An entire social structure is dedicated to holding heterosexuals who marry accountable to one another. Whether it is successful (or ever was) or not, heterosexuals who want to marry or divorce have a process into which they enter. Sometimes it involves counselors or clergy, usually it involves family and friends, and almost always it involves lawyers and the state. As lesbians, we have none of these structures. While I would not advocate needing a lawyer to end each lesbian relationship (picture it!), I do think we need to ask: What does it mean to our relationships that we don't have formal structures for beginning and ending them? Are we more casual about entering into a relationship, I wonder, because there is no possibility of marriage?

When lesbians date, very few people outside of our own community or network wonder if we've just met "Ms. Right." Our relationships can be as casual or intricate as we want to make them, and we frequently opt for casual. Separation for lesbian couples is similar, especially when no children are involved. If we've kept our money and property separate, and there is no social incentive to do otherwise, then separating may be an emotional trauma to one or both of the partners, but there is no requirement for them to reconsider, no waiting period until the separation is final, no public forum in which to divide property and formally recognize that this couple has become two separate individuals. Nothing in our social system seems to visibly hold us accountable for having said to another woman, I love you.

On the other hand, because we are human (in addition to being both women and lesbians) we do belong to a community that calls us to accountability in our relationships: the human community. When we say there is nothing to hold us accountable to one another in our relationships, we are ignoring the larger reality that what we do in our personal relationships affects our community. This accountability has nothing to do with being lesbian and everything to do with keeping some acceptable level of civility and mutuality in all aspects of our lives.

As Marty, the ex-nun, said in an earlier chapter about parents and young children, children have rights and adults have rights and responsibilities. When we're in love, sometimes we lose the balance between those two. Daphne's lover Sheila thought she had a "right" to know everything that Daphne had been doing and know it exactly when Sheila wanted to know it. Her love left no room for Daphne to have rights also.

One thing that works against a system of checks and balances in lesbian relationships is that traditionally we have had to keep our relationships secret. Even today, while so many lesbians are coming out, being public about their personal lives, we know it isn't always safe to live openly. And when we live secretly, accountability suffers. Daphne was closeted at work and had a very closed network of lesbian friends, all of whom were also Sheila's friends. The process of losing her own friends began early in the relationship, as Sheila controlled whom they would see, how often, and under what circumstances, a fairly common factor in a battering relationship. When

Daphne needed to talk about what was happening between her and Sheila, she felt she had no one to turn to. "No one at work knew I was a lesbian. That would be quite an opening, you know, 'Hey, I'm a lesbian and by the way my lover's beating the shit out of me.' If I talked to someone who told Sheila what I said, I'd get hit again. And at that point in our relationship, I didn't know any lesbian Sheila hadn't introduced me to." So she called a therapist and found the independent support she needed.

What happened when Sheila's friends found out that she was using violence in her relationship? Absolutely nothing, Daphne says. "She told them how terrible I was, how I was playing around on her. Which I wasn't. They felt sorry for her. I told a couple of them about the battering. The therapist helped me do that. But I don't think they really believed me."

That scenario does not represent accountability. We owe Sheila that feedback, which would call her to accountability, not because she is a lesbian, but because she is a human being with whom we interact. Furthermore, Sheila is probably not happy about her own behavior—I learned that from the woman I was counseling who used violence to vent her frustration—and yet Sheila has been given no support for changing her behavior, no feedback that it might be undesirable, destructive to her as well as to her lovers. Sheila knows this, at some level, but she is ashamed of her behavior and would rather not acknowledge it. "Oh, it wasn't that bad" is what my friend tried to tell me once after she had slapped her lover's face, knocked her to the ground, and pulled out chunks of her hair. "Yes it is," I told her. "It is bad," and I told her that again and again until she heard it.

Accountability seems like a strange word to use when we talk about love. My credit-card bank holds me accountable for my debts, I try to hold my mechanic accountable for the service he provides to my car—we use the word most often these days in commercial transactions. And yet, at its very source, I believe the word is important to use when we talk about power and relationships. Accountability is about a system of checks and balances that prevent the abuse of power; it is about responsibility, fulfilling obligations to others and ensuring that obligations to us are equally fulfilled. Finally, account-ability is about creating mutuality, the ultimate goal of power sharing.

REFERENCES

1. I don't mean that the effects of heterosexism itself are benign or not harmful. See, for example, Adrienne Rich, "Compulsory Heterosexuality and Lesbian Existence," in *Blood, Bread, and Poetry*, New York: Norton, 1986.

2. Bernice Mennis, "Jewish and Working Class," in *The Tribe of Dina*, ed. Melanie Kaye-Kantrowitz and Irena Klepfisz, Boston: Beacon Press, 1989, p. 330.

3. Steven L. Gortmaker, "Social and Economic Consequences of Overweight in Adolescence and Young Adulthood," *New England Journal of Medicine*, September, 1993, pp. 1008–12.

4. David M. Garner et al., "Cultural Expectations of Thinness in Women," *Psychological Reports*, 4(2), 1980, pp. 483–91.

5. Minnie Bruce Pratt, *We Say We Love Each Other*. San Francisco: Spinsters Ink, 1985, pp. 61–62.

6. "Not So Different, After All: Justice, the Trials of Gay Domestic Violence," *Newsweek* (October 4, 1993), p. 75.

7. Audre Lorde, "The Uses of Anger: Women Responding to Racism," *Sister Outsider*, The Crossing Press, 1984, p. 127.

RESOURCES

Books

Mary Hunt, *Fierce Tenderness: A Feminist Theology of Friendship*. New York: The Crossroad Publishing Co., 1992. Mary Hunt brings a lesbian-feminist perspective to issues of ethics and sexuality, friendship and the limits of friendship, and accountability.

Barbara Sang et al., *Lesbians at Midlife: The Creative Transition*. San Francisco: Spinsters Book Co., 1991. This anthology is one of a kind: articles on getting to midlife and surviving it with dignity. Essays range from the psychological to the political to the purely practical.

PART EIGHT

Uncoupling

The Perfect
Lesbian-Feminist Ending

*L*ike such a thing exists, right? My friend Bernice told me that
her friend Tanya once knew a woman who had actually met a
lesbian (she couldn't remember her name) who was friends with
all of her ex-lovers. And their children. And their present lovers.
Right.

Some lesbians are friends with their ex-lovers. A few are friends
with their ex-husbands. It's nice when it works out like that, but no
matter how virtuous we are during the breakup, no matter how hard
we try to do it right, there are no guarantees. And there is no perfect
ending to a lover relationship. Each ending is its own. I don't see
what is gained by giving our mythical "lesbian who is friends with her
ex-lovers" more credit for her endings than we give to a woman who
has survived a devastating, gut-wrenching breakup.

One of my ex-lovers was a friend before we became lovers and we
are friends again today. Another of my ex-lovers was a total enigma to
me—I was drawn to her in spite of knowing we had nothing in common. We didn't like the same people, the same leisure-time activities,
our politics were diametrically opposite. When whatever was drawing
us together ceased, we still had nothing in common. Today I don't
know her, which is hardly a surprise.

"Maybe I'm missing something," Kathryn, the physical therapist, says earnestly, "but one of my ex-lovers told me I hadn't been a good feminist in how I told her it was finally over." I ask for clarification. "I told her on the phone. She said I should have told her to her face." She is shaking her head as if it still puzzles her. "I mean we talked lots of times about how we really weren't suited and this was just for now. She was still in college and I'd graduated and moved to the city, so it's not like we were in the same town or anything. When she called to make plans, I told her I didn't want to do that. That I thought we ought to end it now. She was furious."

Chances are that Kathryn's ex would have been furious no matter how or how well Kathryn gave her that news. I did a breakup on the phone for my long-distance relationship, and we were both a bit sad, but we knew it was inevitable. She had to stay where she was because of her job, and I knew I didn't want to live in her town. Like Kathryn, we'd talked about the trajectory of our relationship, how it seemed to be heading down to earth, so neither of us was surprised when she called to ask, for the last time, did I want to make a commitment or should she start seeing someone else? I can't make a commitment, I told her, and there was a silence. We both knew what the conclusion would be. Negotiating this on the phone didn't seem particularly unfeminist to me.

"There's no perfect way to do it," insists Leslie. She probably has more ex-lovers than all of the other lesbians in this group combined. Some of her exes are friends, a few call her an enemy, some were casual themselves about the affair, and Leslie can't swear she knew all of their last names. "But their phone numbers," she says, laughing. "I always had a phone number.

"I mean, there are some bad ways to do it, ways that deliberately hurt a woman, and there are some better ways to do it. But perfect? I don't think so."

The bad ways, says Leslie, and I agree, include springing it on her without warning while you're walking out of the bar or club with another woman, telling her it's her fault because she is so . . . (you fill in the blanks), and behaving so badly to her that she finally has to dump you. "That last one can be a bitch. Some women think there's virtue in being dumped, that it makes you the innocent victim, and people will feel sorry for you. But it's much more honorable to take responsibility for what you're feeling and tell her. Just tell her."

Honor and responsibility? Are those part of doing it the better way? "Yeah, sure." Leslie shrugs. "What's the big deal? You have to like a woman well enough to get up close and personal with her. If you like her that much, can't you be honest with her?" Okay. I can see that. But where does the responsibility come into it? "In the beginning," Leslie says without hesitation, "when you set it up. If you know it's going to be casual, you've got a responsibility to say that. Then if it changes, you have to say that too." So the breaking-up is part of the beginning? "It can be. I guess it's part of knowing where you are with the relationship. I get bummed when a woman doesn't know enough about herself to say, like, 'I'd love to have a fling with you, but I know I'll get too caught up in it; it's how I am.'"

Most of the women I talked to about this issue had broken up with at least one someone during their lifetimes, and none could remember a separation that hadn't hurt her and the other woman, no matter how careful and caring they wanted to be. "Usually there are other things that get in there," Marty observes carefully. "Like if my dog had died, my job title was terminated, and then my lover decided to leave—in that order—by the time I got around to dealing with my lover, it was going to be heavy duty, no matter what. My experience is that I store up the hurts, the losses. Oh, not that I don't grieve each one, but there's always some residue left from the one before, and when it's been a recent 'before' it's more than a residue, I can be wading knee-deep through previous muck."

Usually, I find I do things in reverse order. My lover leaves and I fight against feeling that bad about it. I'm upset, but I'll be fine. My job title is redefined, and all of a sudden I'm earning a third less salary and doing twice as much work. I'm getting depressed, but I can cope. Then my dog dies and I flip out. It's safer for me to have feelings about my dog for some reason.

But Marty is right. Emotions aren't simple. Very seldom are we reacting only to the one thing that is happening in our life right now. Each of us has a history of handling loss, anger, grief, rejection, and pain; and this history isn't the same for any two women. No matter how carefully I walk through a breakup with a lover, no matter how lovingly she tells me she no longer wants us to be partners, we can't make it not hurt and we can't be sure that we will still be friends when we are no longer lovers.

The only "good" way I know to separate from a woman I've been loving is to be honest, as hard as that may be. It isn't perfect, but it's better than the alternatives.

Secrets

We were taking a walk one day in February, one sunny day of a winter thaw, when the woman I had been living with for eight years—happily living with, I thought—told me she was unhappy and thinking about a separation. I was stunned. I couldn't believe what I was hearing. Where had this come from? I believed in that moment that I had had no prior warning, that there was nothing in the months past, nothing in our interactions, that would warrant such a step.

I did believe that. Then. Now I know differently. In fact, as soon as I gave it a moment's thought, alone in my study, I knew. We hadn't just been going through the upheaval around a major behavior change on my part (I'd stopped drinking), we were both keeping secrets from one another. I knew she was keeping a secret from me because she *had* to have been thinking about a separation for a long while before she named it to me as something she was ready to do. And I knew I had been keeping secrets from her. One was how angry I was that she could drink "normally" and I couldn't. I was afraid to tell her that, afraid to tell her I didn't want her to drink in our home anymore, afraid that she might want to leave. See. At some level I did know it already.

Beginning to keep secrets from our lovers is one way we begin to separate, begin to end intimate relationships.

No matter how complete my intimacy with the woman who is my lover, I always have things I don't tell her. Not enormous, shattering things, but things about myself I may be dissatisfied with or a little anxious about. Usually I'm not holding back as a conscious choice, it just hasn't come up. "Oh, by the way, dear, have I told you how I hate the way my two front teeth push out?" Not something it's necessary for her to know to understand me, just those details that linger in the crevices of our minds and imaginations to keep us unique.

And there is a difference between privacy and a secret. I am a very private person. There are things about me I don't share easily. But if someone wants to know, needs to know—how it is, for example, that I manage my spiritual life—and if I can tell she's serious in her own searching, I will talk to her about this private matter. It's not a secret. If I won't talk to her about it, in spite of seeing that she is making a serious inquiry, then I'm probably keeping a secret.

When, several months before her amazing pronouncement that she was contemplating a separation, my lover asked me if I'd ever thought about having an affair, I told her no. That was a lie. I lied to preserve a secret, not to maintain my privacy. Privacy doesn't require lying; secrets do.

Finding the secrets in a relationship sometimes can't happen until after the breakup. But if you begin to get a sense that there are secrets between you and the woman you love, secrets that weren't there when your relationship began, then you may have a chance of discovering the real problems that are causing you to separate, to withdraw from intimacy. Some problems can be solved; others are rightly grounds for starting over—with someone else.

Naming the Problem

What is a minor glitch in one relationship may be a monumental roadblock in another. It is amazing to me how easily my friends put up with things in their relationships that would have driven me mad—or away—in the first six weeks. And of course they look at Jan and me and say the same things. How can you stand it when she . . . ?

The differences that Lisa and Mariana experienced when they first began to live together—one of them a morning person, the other a late-night type—could have derailed the relationship if they hadn't found ways of adjusting. Similarly, Barbara might have decided to stay with Susan just long enough to see if she was serious about having a child and then left when the threat became a reality. And Deborah's and Peggy's differing sexual needs could have been a problem so serious that the relationship was in jeopardy.

Kathryn's lover, the one just before Wanda, was an active alcoholic—"Although calling her that seems a little strange, even now, since she was so functional, in most ways." Kathryn was susceptible to falling in love with an alcoholic; it was a family dynamic she was accustomed to, even though she didn't like it. "What seemed comfortable, ironically," she remembers, "is how she would live from crisis to crisis. Not just one or two, but one after the other. I finally realized how familiar this pattern was to me from my mother, and also that she needed a crisis just to know she was alive, to know she could have deep, intense feelings." Kathryn began to be tired of reacting to the crisis of the moment. "Maybe I grew up or something. I just couldn't do it anymore. And she couldn't do without." She shrugs. "Getting out was all I could do."

What makes the difference between a problem that can be managed and one that can't? When have we grown inevitably beyond one another, beyond "fixing" our differences, and when haven't we? For no two couples is the answer the same.

For example, I have a friend, Alex, who is very like me in many significant ways. We joke about how we were both the "overly responsible" ones in our families, taking care of everyone. We're always on time for appointments, our bills are paid on time, when we go hiking I know she will pack enough food for both of us, and so will I. Alex's lover is very different. I have never known her to be on time for anything social, and if they are coming together, I know Alex will do her best, but I plan everything an hour or so later than we've said.

Alex says she admires her lover's ability to be intensely involved in whatever she is doing "in the moment," and the reason she is late is that she hates to leave one wonderful moment even when she knows the next moment will be equally wonderful. This is true about Alex's lover; I've seen it, I've enjoyed her intense focus on me when we have been "in the moment" together. As her lover, I would have lasted about five minutes, but Alex says she doesn't feel disregarded or disrespected by her lover's habitual tardiness.

"That's an attitude," she says, "and I have control of how I look at our difference. She teases me about being compulsive to get to the moment, and I tease her about never wanting to leave the moment."

More than anyone else, of course, Alex has benefited from her lover's intense focus. Her list of wonderful and amazing adventures that have resulted from this odd-fellow partnership include a moonlit walk through Indian Gardens at the Grand Canyon in January because her lover couldn't bear the thought of leaving and they got snowed in. "If we had left when we were scheduled to, we would have missed the snow," Alex admits, but adds adamantly, "but it was one of those life-changing experiences. I've never seen anything so profound in my life." Like I said, it wouldn't suit everyone.

Another friend, in fact, shares a similar difference with her lover. Karen is always on time and feels that honoring appointments and commitments is a way of honoring the person. Her lover, on the other hand, has tremendous anxiety about leaving places. Karen's lover was raised in a military family—one of those who moved every six months or so, uprooting the entire family every time, leaving behind schools, friends, familiar settings, sometimes even the family pets. "It's very hard for her to leave one place and go on to the next," Karen explains, "even when she knows what the next place or event will be. I try to understand this, but when I've been sitting in a restaurant waiting for her for an hour, it's hard not to take it personally."

Karen has a hard time adjusting her attitude because of her own history, both in her family of origin and with previous lovers, of feeling uncared for, ignored. When she feels ignored, her protective response is to withdraw, to distance herself from the hurt. This relationship would have lasted only about a week if Karen weren't getting something else from it. What? "Because I'm the competent one, I'm not used to being taken care of. When my lover says to me, 'Sit down, you've done enough today. I'm going to fix your dinner,' well, I just melt. It astonishes me that she wants to do for me like that." So it's not all one-sided, this relationship. Karen may feel ignored or disrespected when her lover is late for an appointment or doesn't show up at the theater because she got involved somewhere else, but she also has been taken care of, loved, and nurtured.

What keeps these women together, in spite of the stress of their bond? "She's the most fascinating, exciting woman I've ever known," Karen says instantly. And her lover? "Karen moves me in a special way. I've never known anyone like her. She's so intelligent and caring at the same time. And I love her."

There is that. Love. Not always something we can explain. Certainly not something we can discount. When it's there, the struggle is probably worthwhile. When it isn't, maintaining the relationship is harder—both to do and to justify.

For a third couple who experience a similar "time difference," no reconciliation is possible. The lover who is always late feels so criticized and put down by her partner that she doesn't feel loved or loving anymore. For them, it is time to move on.

Naming the problems in a relationship allows us to look at our attitudes. As Alex says, we probably can't change our lovers, but we may be able to change our attitude about how they are, what they do. If we can't love and enjoy them, it's probably time to leave them.

The Nonmonogamy Shuffle

*I*n the fifteenth year of their relationship, when Joan and Marty had been living in separate bedrooms for about five years, but were denying it was over, they opted for nonmonogamy. "We still loved one another," Joan remembers, "and we wanted the relationship to work. But we couldn't figure out what to do about our sex life. Finding sex outside the relationship seemed like a good idea at the time." Was it? "Ha," she snorts. "Not likely. Why should it help? Sex wasn't the problem, it was the result of the problem. The problem was that we didn't trust one another anymore. Me watching Marty make it with another woman, or her watching me find someone to be sexual with, that wasn't really going to help with the trust issues, was it?"

I have to agree. In fact, moving a monogamous relationship to a nonmonogamous one when the relationship is in trouble seems almost guaranteed to speed the ending of the original relationship. Wanda can testify to that. When her lover just preceding Kathryn asked for their relationship to be "open," Wanda agreed. "We were on sort of shaky ground," she remembers, "but the relationship wasn't over. Sex was still great." So what was the shakiness about? "I wanted more time commitment than she did. I wanted to see her a lot. Like every night of the week would have been fine for me. And she wanted to keep it to two nights, three at the most, if there was something special happening."

What happened? "We rationalized that if the relationship was open, I could potentially see someone else a couple of nights a week and get my needs met that way. But instead, she started seeing someone else. I think she used the open-relationship stuff to set up a new lover, someone she could go to when she was done with me. Control stuff. That's what her friends told me. She liked being in control." And surely someone who needed that level of control wouldn't really want her lover involved, however limitedly, with someone else. "No," Wanda agrees. "She wanted me at my home waiting for her. She didn't want me in her house. She just wanted to know where I was."

If a couple begins a relationship with monogamy, not only because they're so into one another the thought of anyone else is ridiculous, but because monogamy suits some deep emotional need of either or both women, then changing the definition of the sexual exclusivity of the relationship is probably not going to help solve problems when they arise. On the contrary, when friends have occasionally told me, sometimes casually, sometimes with pride, that "we've decided to be nonmonogamous" several years into the relationship, what they've usually decided is to end the relationship without telling themselves or one another.

It's Over When . . .

Among lesbians I know, we can generally categorize ourselves as the leavers or the leavees. I've mostly been a leavee, but once or twice I initiated the parting. Jan was usually a leaver, until her most recent relationship before me, when she was left and found out how little she liked that. I didn't like being the leaver any more than I liked being left. It was hard. I worried a lot about what I was doing and how I was doing it.

The difference between being the leaver and the leavee for me was usually one of recognition. I didn't recognize that the relationship was over, so I would hardly have initiated a breakup. I'm not alone in this. Knowing when it's over, when it's time to cut our losses and leave, is not that easy.

One friend found out her relationship was in trouble when she came home late at night after her third business trip in a month and her lover turned to the dog and casually asked, "Who's that, Kelly?" Another friend knew there was something uncomfortable about her relationship, but didn't know what it was. While she and her lover were on vacation at a resort, a woman they had only recently met asked my friend whether she was going to leave her lover after the vacation. "No," my friend replied, astounded. "Why would you ask that?" The woman told her what she'd observed—that her tone of voice when she talked to her lover seemed contemptuous. "You talk about some of her life choices with such scorn in your voice. I was embarrassed for her." My friend insisted that this was her way of joking, that her lover understood where she was coming from. But when they returned home to their daily life, she realized she couldn't put that thought out of her mind. "After a while I had to realize it was true. I didn't respect her," she recalls. "And you can't have a relationship without respect."

The first friend found a new job that let her sleep at home most nights. She, her lover, and the dog are all happy about that. My second friend hasn't found a happy solution. Her relationship ended after thirteen years.

How do we know when it's over?

"When it takes work," says Leslie quickly, "when I'd rather be doing something else, when it isn't fun."

"When I'm getting everything I ask for and there isn't any struggle," says Deborah thoughtfully.

"When she's gone," Marty says ruefully. "That was the only way I could admit it."

"When she's treating you like dirt," insists Ann, "and you know she means for you to do the hard part and kick her out."

"When life takes you in different directions," remembers Joan. "It wasn't that I didn't love her, I just needed something different for my life, something different than she needed."

Whenever. It won't be the same for any two women or for any two couples.

How long does a breakup take? I talked to one woman who may hold the world record. She spent seventeen years breaking up with the same woman. Why, I asked? What was so hard? "I kept trying to figure out why this was happening," she told me, "and what my part in it was. So I wouldn't do it again. I thought there was no point going to another person and doing the same thing wrong again." Well, yes and no. There is a law of diminishing returns, a time when the learning might be more effective in another context. Hanging in there to work on it can be a virtue, or it can be useless. How can we assess the pain and the gain?

"In AA," Marty reminds me, "we have a definition of insanity: doing the same thing over and over and expecting to get different results." Right. To get a different response from a lover, we have to change our input. Too often we've been schooled in the "if at first you don't succeed, try, try again" school of behavior. Especially as women, we tend to think that if a relationship isn't working it's because we forgot something crucial, because we didn't put enough effort into it initially, or because we haven't learned enough yet. Any of these things could be true, but generally, I've found, they're not. Relationships don't work because we're basically incompatible with the woman to whom we've been (inexplicably) drawn. They don't work because we've grown in different directions from the woman we started down the road with. They don't work because we take them too seriously, rarely the opposite.

"I stayed longer than I should have," recalls Daphne, "because I kept thinking *she* would change. I mean, she said she would, that the violence wasn't her usual pattern. I wanted to believe her. So I forgave her. I never tried anything different, like demanding that her behavior change and then forgiving her. I mean, that would have been unique, wouldn't it?" Daphne laughs, half embarrassed at her own question.

She's right, it would have been unique. It is the kind of response few of us think to make in the heat of the moment. Some of us are able to think of such things with the help of a therapist and then go back and confront the moment—when it arises again, which it will—with new direction. Some of us only figure these responses out days or weeks or years after the breakup.

It's probably time to end a relationship when what we've been trying isn't working and we can't think of anything else to try. It's probably time to end a relationship when being with her won't allow you to be your best self. It's probably time to end a relationship when you realize you've been lied to, cheated, trivialized, or physically or emotionally battered. She isn't being her best self in the relationship either, and it's kinder for both of you to end it.

Our Children and Divorce

My first impulse in thinking about this chapter was to say that it's no different from when heterosexuals get divorced; it's hard on everybody and the kids are no exception to that. And then I remembered Bonnie.

I lived with Bonnie's father for four years when I was in my late twenties. About two months after he moved into my apartment, he announced that his wife had called that afternoon, that she was leaving on an extended trip, and his daughter would be coming to live with us for a while. Bonnie lived with me until I left her father four years later. I stayed in the relationship with him longer than I might have because I grew to love the little five-year-old girl who'd arrived on my doorstep with her kitten Twinkletoes and not much else. I knew that leaving her father meant I would no longer have any access to Bonnie. One of her biological parents would have had to grant me that access, would have had to value my contact with her enough to help me see her; and I knew that neither of them would do that for me. I did manage to see Bonnie once, about a year after I left her father. By then I was living with a woman. He never returned my calls again, and my letters to Bonnie went unanswered. I had no recourse.

Basically, this is true for every lesbian who becomes a nonbiological parent. In the end, without a legal adoption, we have no rights. Or almost none. We are truly dependent on the kindness of the biological

(or legal) parents of the children we have been parenting for a continued relationship with those children. And this is true whether we
make the decision together to conceive a child or whether a woman
enters a relationship with another woman who has children. Because
we cannot legally marry, there is no system in place to help us separate; and while that system of divorce for heterosexuals can be horri-
bly oppressive at times, it does ensure that both parents of a child get
a hearing about custody, visitation rights, child support, and other
issues affecting the children.

Some lesbians have told me that is fine with them; they'd rather
rely on the kindness of their partners, or former partners, even under
the stress of ending a relationship, than on the alleged impartiality of
a court. That's a practical attitude to take, since at this time we don't
have many other options.[1] There are some steps we can take when the
relationship is secure that might not guarantee "the best interests of
the child," but they will take us a long way toward a fair settlement.

One option is to work out in advance the who, what, where for
your child (children) fairly early in the relationship. Barbara and
Susan did this when Susan found out she was actually pregnant. "I
knew that Barbara didn't want any responsibility at that point in our
relationship," Susan explains, "and I needed to have somebody who
would take over if something happened to me. Several friends agreed
to be godmothers before Darien was even born." Susan wasn't worried
about a legal scenario as much as she was concerned that someone
she trusted, a lesbian she trusted, be watching over the decisions that
were made about her child. Since there was no biological father of
record in Susan's case, and since her mother was named as guardian
in Susan's will, she knew the role this godmother would play was
largely advisory. Another friend went through a breakup with her
lover when the daughter they had decided to have together was only
three. "It was terrible," she told me. "I wanted to get on with my life,
start over, you know, put the ugliness behind me. But there was
Shana's other mother. I couldn't get a breather. I always had to be
dealing with her about schedules and money." After leaving furious
notes for one another, a series of telephone-call hangups, and other

unhappy confrontations, they finally found a mediator to help them with those kinds of details until the emotional intensity of the breakup diminished somewhat. Today they are both in other relationships and handle the scheduling themselves. "It's easier now that she's in school," my friend says, relieved. "After school on Thursday, she goes to her other mother's house and comes home here on Saturday afternoon. We only have to see each other once a week, and that's the time we talk about money, clothes, schedules. You know, all the stuff you have to figure out."

"You're assuming the other person wants to have a role in the child's life," Ann, who's now a grandmother, accused me. "That wasn't the case for me. Nancy and I bought the ranch together when Sally was thirteen. Sal looked up to her. They were closer in age, and Nancy was gorgeous. A real case of hero worship. Sal had moved out by the time Nancy left, but she was still devastated. Nancy never called her, never sent her a birthday card. It was like Sally had never been a part of her life. I hated Nancy for that more than for leaving me. I couldn't protect Sally from it."

It's true. We can't protect our children from losing someone they've loved any more than we can protect ourselves. This condition exists for all children everywhere—whatever the sexual orientation of their parents—when the adults they love don't love one another anymore.

Trying Again

I will never," moaned my friend, "never ever ever have another lover who . . . "

You fill in the blanks.

. . . who is a writer.

. . . who has children. Who wants children.

. . . who works nights. Who works twelve-hour shifts. Who doesn't work.

. . . who is a middle child. The oldest child. The only child.

. . . who is in a twelve-step program. Who is recovering. Who isn't recovering yet.

We set up guidelines in our moments of desperation that we *ought* to pay attention to when our hormones start raging again. Sometimes we do, sometimes we don't. But almost all of us do start over, we do begin a new relationship, even if it takes a long time.

I was surprised at how long it took me to feel that I might want to be "coupled" with a woman after the breakup of my first major relationship. Not that I didn't try, not that I didn't date, not that I didn't have lovers, but whenever we got close to that moment of decision (and usually I didn't let it even get close), I pulled back. That didn't surprise me the first few years after the breakup. I had a lot of work to do: I moved into a new community, I was shifting my employment emphasis. Who had time to get serious, I asked myself? In the fourth and fifth years, I began to wonder if my scars were really that deep. Maybe I'd missed something? And so I went into therapy with a woman who specialized in grief work. I talked about losing my mother, my lover, and my grandmother in a few short years. Definitely I had some material to work on, I realized. By the sixth and seventh years, when I still wasn't feeling drawn to any woman I wanted to settle in with, I began to talk with friends about the benefits of being single, about how I could find the intimacy I wanted, the daily sharing, without having a live-in lover. Being single was beginning to seem normal and satisfactory to me. I liked my life a lot.

That was how I felt when I met Jan. I wasn't looking for a partner, I didn't feel deprived by the life I was living, but there she was, and within a short time I wasn't single anymore.

"I never thought I'd try again," says Ann, half embarrassed at the admission that she has indeed found a partner at this time in her life. "And I wasn't even that hard to convince." She sounds as though that's even harder to believe.

"Of course I'll be with another woman someday," says Susan softly, a few weeks after Barbara's death. "I loved Barbara, I loved being with her. It's one way of honoring the good times we had together to say I hope I'll have that with another woman. And have it fairly soon."

"I've always pretty much known who I'd be with before I left the last lover," confesses Daphne. "If I lost Leslie, though? I don't know. That might be different."

"No," says Joline. "I can't imagine being with anyone if I weren't with Sarah."

"I hope I'll be with someone again sometime," admits Marty, "but I've got a lot of work to do before I'm ready. I've only been sober for a year. Joan and I've only been separated for a year. I'm forty-six, but I feel like a kid. Ask me again in two or three years, okay?"

Okay. We *can* do the work. We *can* be ready to try again. But it is, basically, a question that only life will answer for us.

REFERENCE

1. April Martin, *The Lesbian and Gay Parenting Handbook*, New York: Harper-Collins, 1993, pp. 152–53. Second-parent adoptions are legal in only a few states at this time, but it seems a very promising avenue for legalizing a nonbiological parent's relationship with a child.

PART NINE

Going Long Term

How Long Is Long Term?

When I began this book, I was in my forties. My forties. It sounds like a fairly safe age, mature but not old. During the writing of the book, I turned fifty, so now I'm in my fifties. This no longer seems such a safe place. My mother died in her fifties. I lost a good friend a few weeks after she turned fifty. The future seems a little shorter than it did last year.

As with age, what we know or think we know about long-term relationships depends a bit on where we're viewing them from. At twenty, a long-term relationship was two or three years. Any couple who had made it to a third anniversary was quite extraordinary. At thirty, I began the longest relationship of my life, and I expected it to last forever. When we had our fifth anniversary, we were surrounded by couples about our age with similar histories and longevities. When we had our seventh, we were more unusual. Before our ninth anniversary, we broke up. Those few couples who went on to celebrate their tenth, then fifteenth, awed me. I wanted that for my life, but it didn't seem possible.

Today I know lesbian couples who have been together for twenty-five or thirty-five years. In heterosexual marriages of that length, we occasionally hear that one or both partners "stayed for the children" long after the relationship or any mutual affection had vanished. That simply isn't true of most of the lesbian couples I know. They are together because they want to be, because they still find delight and surprises in one another, because they basically like (as well as love) and are liked by their partners.

And yet I have also known one or two couples who, like Joan and Marty, after fifteen or so years as an "ideal" couple in the eyes of their community, admit it wasn't so great after all. In Clare Coss's study of single lesbians, one woman voices this other point of view:

> Somebody who's been in a long relationship is stranger in the gay life than people who've been in and out of them. . . . Somebody comes along and breaks them up and they're ready to break up and there's a catalyst and then you hear they never had sex, they never got along, they never did this, they never did that. I always think the very long relationships have been: "Let's not risk what's out there. This is steady." I think the longest one I ever had went on because we bought a house together.[1]

But what about those women who have "made it" in long-term relationships? What made it work? What is there to learn for all of us who want or expect our relationships to last, to give us satisfaction for a long, long time? For all of us who want to grow within a relationship, rather than as a result of learning from each relationship we've lost?

The Comfort Factor

*T*hey *like* each other a lot, these two women who are sitting across from me in the retirement/nursing home. They're both nearly eighty (they won't say their exact ages) and they've lived together for forty-five years. Sharon was born in a tightly cohesive Jewish immigrant community in Chicago sometime after World War I, and her partner, Nan, was raised on a farm in Iowa. I've heard their stories—how Sharon went to Los Angeles and was living the "life" during the thirties and forties with a few lesbian friends and dozens of gay men, how Nan was a schoolteacher in Iowa until World War II, how they met as Red Cross volunteers during the war, fell in love, and began their marriage shortly after the war ended. Today Nan has severe degenerative osteoporosis. She is in continual pain and unable to do much for herself. When all of the cooking and cleaning became too much for Sharon, they agreed to move into this home. It offers progressive care: independent elders have their own apartments with meals and nursing care available as needed; actual nursing-home care is also available when independent living isn't possible. The home didn't make any fuss at all, Nan and Sharon tell me, about two women sharing an apartment.

"Did I tell you how wonderful this girl is?" Nan asks me, gesturing toward Sharon. The details aren't important. Her tone of voice is. Sharon is shaking her head with pleased embarrassment. When Nan goes on to tell me about some incident from their past to emphasize her point, Sharon is quiet until Nan asks, "What year was that, now?" And Sharon remembers it was the same year they made their trip to Israel, right after Nan retired from teaching full time. "That's right," Nan agrees. "It was 1977."

Live-in intimacy. Many times I've asked myself if it is worth the work. Part of my answer is here in this small retirement apartment. Nan and Sharon reflect the joy they have experienced in one another over the years. It is not that they finish one another's sentences. They don't. They do refer to one another's memory of the past as though it were a common memory bank, which in many respects it is. They have faced life together and found comfort in that. Not only are these two women comfortable together, the very presence of the other is comforting to each of them.

After talking with Sharon and Nan, I decide to call Susan, whose partner of eleven years, Barbara, died two months ago from ovarian cancer. "That is a major part of living with someone for a long time," she agrees, "if it's working, that is. It took us several years to get through some of the frictions." She pauses. "More than several, actually. It was about the time Darien went to preschool, about our sixth year together, that it seemed like it just got easier. We knew what to expect from one another. And at some level, I knew we were together for life—whatever that meant to me before we found out about Barbara's cancer. We'd done the tough stuff, you know? And she hadn't bolted then. I hadn't either. So why shouldn't we go on, once it had gotten comfortable."

But I'm asking about more than comfortable, I explain. Did it comfort you that she was there? "I hadn't thought about it in those terms," Susan replies slowly, "but, yes, even if I was the one getting up because Darien had an earache, and I had to decide whether his temperature was high enough to go racing off to the emergency clinic or whether it could wait until morning, I knew I wasn't alone. If I needed help I could get it. And when I went back to bed, I knew I'd get a hug, a snuggle, her arms around me." That's comfort.

"Oh, yes," agrees Margaret, when I ask her about comfort in her twenty-five-year relationship with Rachel, "I think I began to understand it about the fifteenth year." It took that long? I'm sort of laughing, but Margaret is serious. "Yes, actually. We had a lot of ups and downs. Remember, I told you about Rachel's enthusiasms?" I do remember. "Well, every now and then one of her projects she'd get excited about would carry her pretty far away from me. It took me that long to trust that she'd be back, that I was her anchor." Who was Margaret's anchor in this configuration? "I didn't need one." She laughs now. "I had both feet stuck firmly in the mud until I met Rachel. She was the bounce in my life. At least that's what I thought. After she died," Margaret shrugs, remembering, "after the accident, I thought my life was over too. But I'd learned enough from Rachel. It had rubbed off. I could find my own things to get enthusiastic about."

The comfort in this relationship, explains Margaret, was trusting that Rachel would be back and enjoying the space her absence created as well as the excitement of her return. "I think the hardest thing about the last seven years, being alone, is not having someone to share the wonderful moments with. Not that she has to be there for each one of them, but when something funny or outrageous or wonderful happens, I have someone who wants to hear about it." Margaret and Ann store these gems up for one another, she tells me, and part of their coming-together ritual after a separation is sharing these moments.

In my own life, I am only beginning to understand again what it means to have someone who is there, a lover who is with me differently than even my closest friends. Since we became lovers and began living together, Jan and I have both lost our fathers. While we had very different relationships with them as fathers, the intense family events of illness, death, and funerals are inevitable. She tells me that my presence at her side when she visited her father for the last time and when we went to his funeral was important to her, useful and comforting. When my dad was hospitalized during his last illness and we had just driven home from visiting him, only to receive a call that he'd had another crisis, it was Jan who said, at eleven o'clock at night, "We'll go back." Not having to go alone and not having to ask for help, that is what comfort means to me.

Illness and the Relationship

The last ten years, says a friend in her sixties, have been one medical crisis after another for her and her lover. Another woman in my community speaks out at a gay and lesbian event: her partner of twenty years has been ill for the last eight years and they feel cut off, abandoned by the community. Two lesbians in their seventies, partners for thirty-five years, try to go to some lesbian social events and are made to feel unwelcome by the younger, forty-fifty-ish lesbians because they talk so much about their pain and ill health. Another lesbian, open about her own sexuality, has lived for twenty-two years with her very closeted lover, who has recently been diagnosed with MS. Their rather delicately balanced situation has become nearly impossible as a result of this illness, which requires more support than they can expect from a tiny circle of friends who know about their relationship.

Relationships that go long term are more likely to encounter illness or medical crisis. When these are lesbian relationships, many factors can make dealing with such a crisis very, very difficult. We rely on one another as couples at these times, and we would rely on our families and communities too, if we could define them, if they knew we were a couple, if we had previous relationships that were supportive within our families and communities.

When we have only ourselves as couples to rely on, the stress can become overwhelming.[2] Those couples I've talked with who had good family and community support before illness became a problem were able to go through the crisis, in most cases, rather than become mired in it.

Barbara and Susan found out about Barbara's ovarian cancer in the eighth year of their relationship, at a time when they had settled into their life together, assuming that they would be family for a long time. Barbara's daughter, Jeanie, was in her first year of college in a neighboring state—distant enough to give the couple some extra space, close enough to come home for an occasional weekend and holidays. Darien had just started first grade. Their new business as self-employed carpenters was beginning to flourish. But most importantly, Barbara and Susan had worked actively to make a cohesive lesbian community in their rather isolated rural neighborhood.

"We knew about thirty or forty lesbians in a fifty-mile radius," says Susan. "They'd been to our home or we'd been to theirs, mostly for social events, picnics, that sort of thing. But some of us were interested in being more informed about political things that might affect us, so we'd had some meetings, too, and gotten to know one another pretty well. When Barbara was going through chemo, there were about six women who helped out, either staying here with Darien while I went to the hospital with her, or driving her there, or to a doctor's appointment. I don't know how I would have gotten through it without them." Even with all that support, Susan was "living on an edge of exhaustion and anxiety" most of the two years of Barbara's illness. She and Barbara had no disability insurance and so Susan had to try to keep the business going, take care of her son, be a comfort to Barbara's daughter, and be there in whatever way Barbara needed. "I think I averaged about three hours of sleep a night during that last year and a half."

Barbara and Susan had invested in health insurance for themselves through a community group of self-employed business owners. All of Barbara's medical expenses were covered by the insurance, although the extras they needed—like day care and drivers—were not. "We thought it was kind of crazy at the time," remembers Susan, "buying a policy that cost so much. Our premiums for two adults and two children were over $250 a month. Basically, I wanted it for Darien. I wanted a doctor I could take him to before he got really sick, and I knew I wouldn't do that if I had to pay $60 or $70 for each visit. So we signed up for an HMO that was $2 per visit. Darien's barely used it." She smiles ruefully. "I never had time to think about taking him to the doctor while Barbara was ill."

What would they have done without the medical insurance? "I have no idea," says Susan. "Probably we'd have had to sell the house and cars, maybe even the van we use for the business, before she would have been covered by the state. Nothing we own would have bought the medical services we used in the first year of her illness. That was over $100,000 with the surgery and chemotherapy treatments and all."

The two factors Susan has identified that made it possible for her to cope during Barbara's illness and then to go on afterward are having a supportive lesbian community they built up over the years and having medical insurance.

The other factor is less definable, something that happened between her and Barbara during their last two years together. Susan calls it a gift, but she isn't sure how to describe it. "We grew so much closer, especially toward the end. I guess that isn't a surprise, but it showed me . . . " She pauses, searching for words. "I don't want this to sound wrong. But it showed me some things that had been missing earlier in our relationship. We gained a level of closeness and intimacy that I almost think we never would have achieved. It's changed me in ways that are pretty profound. I'll never want less, as far as that emotional intimacy goes, in any kind of partner relationship I might have in the future."

There is one other positive thing that came out of this sad time, Susan tells me. "It's the kind of change you go through when you're dealing with a life-threatening illness. You learn to appreciate each day for what it is, the joys of each day. You don't take things for granted. This spring, I've been so much more aware of all the green things. I guess I'm more aware of the blessings I do have."

Sandra and Beth are another couple who have recently had to deal with illness in the relationship. Eight months ago, Sandra, who is thirty-six, had a hysterectomy. The primary effect they have felt in the relationship was in regard to their sex life. "Before I decided to have the operation, I went through nearly a year of bleeding heavily all the time." Sandra sighs at the memory. "Finally, we were both totally frustrated. I mean, if I had a few days when I wasn't bleeding, we would make love. Sometimes. If I wasn't too tired. I'm not talking about just having a period, you know, I mean massive bleeding. It does put a damper on sex." Beth agrees, mostly. "I felt like Sandra's exhaustion was the major problem, though. What energy she had she gave to the kids. We'd fall into bed at night and she'd be asleep before I could even turn over toward her. I thought the hysterectomy wasn't the best idea, but it was the only option we had at that point."

Now, eight months postsurgery, I ask them how their sex life is—not an easy question for them. Beth is waiting for Sandra to tell me about it. "I'm not as tired as I was," she says slowly, "but I don't have much desire, either. Orgasms aren't the same when you don't have a uterus to contract." She shrugs that off. "But it's more than that. I just don't feel sexual. I don't know why or what happened. My doctor said it wouldn't affect my sex life. But what did she know? She still had her uterus."

"We're trying to treat this as normal," Beth adds now. "We're thinking about it as recovery still, and part of the process of recovery, we hope, will be Sandra's sexual desire. We've talked to some women who've been through this, and they all told us it would come back." In the meantime, Beth can be understanding and Sandra can try to be responsive. It isn't the best solution, they say, but it's all they can do for now.

While menopause is not an illness, it does sometimes carry with it symptoms that are difficult for individual women and for the couple. And lesbian couples have the added pressure of knowing they will be going through menopause not once but twice, since it's a hers and hers situation.

Fortunately, menopause is not the same for every woman, although we all experience it to some degree or another. A friend whose lover went through a terrible series of symptoms during menopause—three years of intense hot flashes, mood swings that were debilitating and frightening, energy loss—was terrified of her own approaching menopause. "I worried about it for years," she said, "and then it was here and gone. Nothing to write home about. My period was over for two years before I actually believed I was done, that it had been that easy."

Many lesbians report the pleasure of finishing with menstruation, the increase of energy and focus and renewed sexual vigor. Hoping to hear those stories, when my partner and I began experiencing our first symptoms of menopause (within a year of each other), we started asking our friends who were our ages or older how it had been with them. To our dismay, most said, Oh, it isn't a problem, I'm on hormone replacement.

While hormone-replacement therapy may be important for some women's sense of well-being, Jan and I view menopause and the cessation of estrogen production as normal to a woman's physical life. For us, hormone replacement isn't one of the options in dealing with our own symptoms of menopause. Through our acupuncturist and naturopathic physician, we have found vitamins and herbs that are useful in easing this transition of our bodies into another physical age. We are fortunate to live in an area where these forms of treatment are available.

But hiking has perhaps been our own most effective version of hormone therapy. When either of us gets moody or anxious, when life seems too closed in, when we're tired and nothing seems quite right, we try to schedule a long hike.

Our relationship *has* been affected by passing through menopause. We were fairly new lovers when Jan's first hot flashes began, and her inability to sleep through a night was hard on us both. More difficult still were mood swings and feelings she did not understand, partly because she could not even identify the emotions. Because we didn't have a long history with one another, we couldn't predict the other's behavior at these times. She wondered whether she should be alone until she felt better, rather than inflict these moods on me. I wondered if she would leave, if I had done something wrong, if this time would pass. Basically, all we could do was wait and trust the feelings we expressed to one another during our commitment celebration. It worked. But it left me wondering how other lesbian couples—newly together or old-timers—have weathered this awesome transition.

Aging and the Relationship: The Opening Out

"Oh, yes," says my eighty-something friend Sharon, "it's so much easier being gay, you know, than it was when we were younger." Is that because of changing times, I ask, or because you are older? "Well, I would have to say it's a bit of both. Wouldn't you, Nan?"

Nan is nodding agreement. "I'd have to say it got a lot easier for me when I retired. I never hid that I lived with Sharon, but I was very careful how I talked about her." Nan, of course, was an elementary-school teacher for fifty years, and her hesitations were probably well founded. The only people who knew about their relationship in those years before Nan's retirement were other gay couples, all of them men. "We never seemed to find any other women who wanted to know us. They were afraid, I think, the few we did hear about."

Sharon's work life was almost entirely around men. She began as a secretary, but soon her facility with numbers and her love of accounting sent her in that direction. Without any formal education beyond high school, Sharon worked in banks, first in California and then, after the war, in the Midwestern town she and Nan settled in. "Today there are all sorts of women working at that level in banks, probably even some gay girls," she says, "but when I began, the departments I worked in, well, it was all men. And that wasn't where the gay fellows were, either."

They watched the beginnings of this wave of feminism with avid interest, particularly the struggles between straight feminists and the radical lesbians. They subscribed to the first issue of *Ms.* magazine and several of the new journals after that. "We particularly liked the music," confides Nan. "We went to some of the coffeehouse concerts they held here in town. After I retired, that is. The younger women never acted like we shouldn't be there. We were just part of the crowd." Attending these concerts "outed" Nan and Sharon to a limited community, and for the last ten years they've enjoyed knowing a few lesbian couples in their forties and fifties.

It is especially nice, they explain, being at a place in their lives where it doesn't matter so much what people think of them. And, yes, it is also true that many people are more open to the lesbian lifestyle these days.

Ann and Margaret, the couple in their sixties, have only been together a short time, but both find age to be a positive factor in their relationship. "Things that used to tie me up in knots just aren't so important anymore," admits Margaret. Like what, I wonder? "Like having to be the one who drives the car when Ann and I go out. Like eating dinner in a restaurant that falls short of wonderful. Those things really used to bother me." She laughs. "Either I'm mellowing or my standards are shot to hell."

Ann's experience of aging is different, but also important to her. More like Sharon and Nan, Ann is finding herself relieved not to have to be so closeted. "Oh, sure, some of those old fogies in the place where I live would have a heart attack if they found out I was gay," she says, "and some of them are just fine with it. The difference is in me. It doesn't bother me. Nothing can happen to me except they won't like it. I won't lose my job. My daughter won't be bugged at school." She shrugs. "Who cares what they think?"

In private, Margaret has told me it's a good thing Ann is less concerned about being out than she used to be, because for Margaret being out is a way of life. "I've always hated hiding who I am and who

I love. It's why I've been self-employed all these years. I never would have lasted a minute working for some company that told me how I could live."

Sarah and Joline, while only in their thirties, are a couple whose relationship has lasted twenty years and is still growing and vital. They, no less than Nan and Sharon, feel that their own aging process has affected their relationship positively. "Thank heavens," says Joline. "It's a good thing. I mean, we had to grow up. We were kids when we started. But I'll say it's a relief to have been through all those stages we've been through and feel like now we know who we are—we're lesbians—and we aren't afraid to say the word." To one another, anyway. And who knows, as Sarah and Joline keep opening out in this aging process, they may find themselves saying the word to a wider and wider circle of friends, family, and acquaintances.

Aging and the Relationship: Managing the Transitions

Do I have a retirement annuity plan or life insurance?" Leslie looks at me as if I'm crazy to be asking this question, and I wonder if she thinks it's outrageously stupid to be thinking about such a thing when you're thirty years old. "Of course I do. It was one of the first things I set up when I got out of school." Oh, right. Leslie's M.B.A. "I made sure Daphne had one, too. We'd like to retire when we're fifty. Travel. Maybe start our own business. Daphne's talked about doing some import stuff, having her own shop down in Key West or someplace like that. We aren't going to live in Detroit the rest of our lives, you can count on that. We've got plans."

How we, as couples, manage some of the transitions that come with age has a great deal to do with planning for those transitions. Barbara's death was an unwelcome transition for Susan, and yet they were able to cope with the moment because they'd done some planning around medical insurance. For Joan and Marty, the transition was about work—Marty wanting to begin a private counseling practice at home, where Joan was running a bed-and-breakfast. Their planning for the transition included a lot of discussion about how they would both be in the house together for that much time, in addition to the more obvious discussion about money. It wasn't this transition that led to the failure of Joan and Marty's relationship; the transition was well planned.

"Oh, you can plan all you want," Sharon's sharp voice contradicts me, "but the most important things about it you can't predict." She is talking about her own retirement. "We'd waited years to be able to travel as much as we wanted," she tells me. "And we'd planned, yes, we'd planned. The money was there. We knew where we wanted to go. And we did." The problem? "I didn't want to retire. I wasn't *ready* to retire."

Nan, who is three years younger than Sharon, wasn't scheduled to retire until 1977, but the bank where Sharon had worked for the last twenty years told her, not so gently, that she would be retiring in 1974. "We thought that would be fine," says Nan, "because I was a teacher and had summers off. We had three European summers planned, and then as soon as I retired we were off to Israel for a winter." The problem? "What was Sharon going to do with herself during the rest of the year? Every morning that first month she was like a racehorse at the starting gate, but they never opened the doors. I never saw anything like it. If it had been me . . . " She shakes her head reflectively. "I love to garden and sew. I had a thousand projects in mind for retirement. Sharon isn't the project type," she adds unnecessarily. "I felt like she was starting to hate me, every time I went out the door to school."

"Oh, it wasn't like that," Sharon protests. But she agrees she was starting to hate herself. "I felt useless, totally useless, and I never expected that. I didn't have the kind of job like Nan's where I *mattered* to people, like she did to those children. Anybody could have done the work I was doing."

Sharon thought about a part-time job, but that seemed silly since it would just about equal the Social Security check she was getting by not working. It was a pretty tense six months, they tell me.

Did they ever think of breaking up? Ending the relationship? "Oh, no." They look at me horrified. "Why would we have done that?" I explain that in my research I've found couples who felt something was wrong in one of their lives and the solution seemed to be to start over with someone new. Usually it didn't help, since the problem wasn't generated by the relationship, but the relationship got blamed, since it wasn't solving the problem. Sharon and Nan nod, seeming to understand, but Sharon asks the most obvious question. "Where would I have gone? I was sixty-six years old."

Sharon ended up going back to school, not for a degree, she explains, but for some of the cultural education she'd missed by not going to college. "I decided feeling useless was a state of mind and that I'd better get over it. Taking an art history course didn't make me feel useful, it just got me interested in things I'd always enjoyed but didn't understand much. It made our European trip that summer seem like a field trip for what I'd been studying."

Flexibility. The willingness to change attitudes that aren't helpful. These are the things that make relationships work whether we're in our twenties, forties, or eighties. The transitions we can control, to some extent, are the psychological and social ones. Most of the lesbians I interviewed for this study, particularly the older women, have the psychological flexibility to deal with much of what life offers. We've had to, after all, set our own standards for things heterosexuals take for granted—things like morality, commitment, and even fulfillment. Finding our way as older lesbians in a culture that doesn't value old age is less problematic for us, I think, than for heterosexuals. Mainstream culture never valued lesbianism either. But we have. We've made our own values. We know how to do this.

Aging also means retirement, a social transition, for most of us in this culture, although I have a few friends who insist they will keep working until they die. Lesbians, as a group, are vulnerable to becoming impoverished "older" women when we retire because many of us, like Margaret, don't work within a corporate system. Relying on Social Security to cover those retirement years when we won't be working for an income isn't a good idea, nor is relying on our ability to keep working until we drop dead. If we didn't start our own retirement fund, like Leslie, the minute we left college, what are our options?

Not all lesbians are middle class or professional class, but I have heard some who are financially well off talking about creating communities of inclusive self-help for all older lesbians. Others see lesbian-managed nursing homes as essential. Whether these projects are created or not, lesbians have always aged, whether we've wanted to or not, whether we've been prepared or not, and most of us have relied on the help of our partners, of a few close friends, to manage this transition. As the lesbian community continues to open out in the nineties, and on into the twenty-first century, our political agenda must include provisions for older lesbians.

I will be sixty-five in the year 2008. When I saw that date on my pension plan in 1972, the first year I started teaching college full time and was offered a chance to buy into the college teachers' retirement plan, I laughed. I was twenty-nine years old. I couldn't imagine a year when I'd be wanting a pension. "Do it anyway," said my father, and I did. Today, 2008 doesn't seem so far away. The pension I have accrued with my erratic history of teaching doesn't seem like much, but I'm glad it is there. As I said earlier, the future seems closer every year now.

Aging has transitions in store for us that are not psychological or social; and they're not about illness either. Aging is a physical process that changes our bodies. Our metabolism slows, our muscles will lose flexibility if we don't keep moving them, our bones can lose density if we don't use them, sometimes they will lose density no matter what we do.

"I'm slowing down," admits Marty, who is only forty-six. "It's not a lot, but I don't recover as quickly as I did, even five years ago." Recover? "From a long hike or a late night out dancing. Any kind of physical expenditure. The storehouse doesn't replenish as quickly as it used to." Marty doesn't find this slowing down a problem; she's adjusted fairly easily, in fact, to letting herself have an extra day after a hike, a late morning after a night of dancing.

But many lesbians I talked with said they were in better physical shape in their forties and fifties, particularly, than they'd ever been before in their lives. "I don't know what it is, exactly," said a friend who is a therapist. "Maybe it's just the fitness thing the whole culture seems to be going through. But I'm out biking every other day and I feel great. I've lost ten pounds, and my breathing is a hundred percent easier than the first time I went out on a bike." Another woman said she'd recently taken up Rollerblading. When she went into the store to buy a set of in-line skates, the clerk took one look at her gray hair and asked if she wanted them for her grandson. "You can believe I told him what for," she says. "After all, I'm only sixty-three."

I look at pictures of my mother when she was my age, and although she led an active life, she looked—at fifty—a great deal older than I look at fifty. Part of it's style. I don't cut my hair in a matronly style. I mostly wear blue jeans and sweatshirts. I don't think my mother ever owned a pair of blue jeans. Some of it's attitude. I resist thinking of myself as a responsible middle-class citizen.

Nonetheless, aging will happen. We may age a little more slowly than our parents. We may understand better how to keep our bones from growing porous and brittle. We may never be ill a day in our lives. And yet we will age. Our partners will age. We will become the next generations' foremothers. They will look at our relationships, our partnerships, to see what they can learn about themselves and their own lives.

REFERENCES

1. Clare Coss, "Single Lesbians Speak Out," in *Lesbians at Midlife*, ed. Barbara Sang, Joyce Warshow, and Adrienne J. Smith. San Francisco: Spinsters Book Co., 1991, p. 134.

2. Judith Bradford and Caitlin Ryan, "Who We Are: Health Concerns of Middle-Aged Lesbians," in *Lesbians at Midlife*, pp. 147–63. This report from the National Lesbian Health Care Survey contains important statistics and information on many subjects, including the ways in which closeting of older lesbians makes health care support more difficult. One of the most common concerns was economic viability in old age.

Index